the food junctions cookbook
living recipes for social innovation

First published as the *Food Junctions Cookbook* in 2011
by Marina Chang and Lukas Meusburger

University College London
Gower Street, London
WC1E 6BT, United Kingdom

The recipes presented in this *Cookbook* have not been tried or tested by the editors, who cannot guarantee their performance and safety.

ISBN 978-0-9570354-0-9

British Library Cataloguing in Publication Data.
A catalogue record for this book is available from the British Library.

Design and drawing: Chris Lemmens - twisted carpet
Printed and bound by Calverts Co-operative

RECYCLED
Paper made from
recycled material
FSC
www.fsc.org   FSC® C007915

Free PDF download at www.food-junctions.org.uk

the food junctions cookbook
living recipes for social innovation

edited by
marina chang
lukas meusburger

Contents

Acknowledgements

Throughout this journey we have been supported by many people without whose help and advice this project would not have been possible. We would like to express our gratitude to all of those involved in this journey, whose willingness to share their experiences, stories, wisdom and insights helped develop this *Cookbook*.

We were never alone, optimism and enthusiasm coming from working with our core team members at *Food Junctions*: Regan Koch, Julian Cox, Shuen-Yi Long, Stephanie Mills, Lucy Natarajan, Ailbhe Gerrard and Sharon Tan – thank you very much for getting the project started in the first place. Thanks also go to Daniel Fitzpatrick, Michael Stuart and Karol Yanez at *Foodpaths* who helped continue this challenging but always joyful journey.

We are grateful to the UCL Public Engagement Unit - Steve Cross, Hilary Jackson and Gemma Moore - for supporting a group of students at all levels and enabling us to run large projects like ours. Their panel not only financed *Food Junctions* and *Foodpaths* and the major part of this *Cookbook*, but the team also helped us solve many problems along the way. Helpful sums were also contributed by a grant from the UCL Grand Challenge of Sustainable Cities and the Engineering and Physical Sciences Research Council (EPSRC). Few could hope for a better place to gain such enormous institutional support than UCL, and thanks are due to all there, particularly Michael Worton, Sally MacDonald, Ian Scott, Clare Ryan, Robert Eagle, Rachel Lister and John Braime.

'Be the change you want to see in the world'.
Mahatma Gandhi

Front Quad, UCL

We would like to extend our thanks to Phil Paulo at Camley Street Natural Park and Louise Gates at the Calthorpe Project for letting us experiment with our ideas and use their venues for the *Food Junctions* and *Foodpaths* events respectively. They, along with many other community groups and individuals, have taught us that there are lots of recipes for good and exciting university and community collaborations but the ingredients must always include empathy and kindness. We need a vision and the big picture as well as attention to detail and hard work. Fun and food are definitely useful. We have also learnt that accepting that we are all different while at the same time focusing on our common interests is a good start.

Our heartfelt thanks go to the contributors of this collection who took time to write essays based on faith that this book would really happen, and whose wonderful pieces made the work of putting this *Cookbook* together truly enjoyable. Thanks for bearing with our many queries and not being annoyed by our chasing up questions about the article, image or copyright forms, even after midnight sometimes. Thanks to Harry West for supporting our events and his beautiful 'mistake' of forwarding our invitation to him to contribute a piece to the entire SOAS Food Studies Centre mailing list. As a result, we received a number of contributions from this network.

Thanks to Ian Fitzpatrick, who helped us

fulfil our goal of making these seventy-three very different contributions look like part of a whole while also keeping their own voices and remaining faithful to what the author meant and intended. Special thanks go to the two graphic designers – Adriana Molina and Chris Lemmens – for *Food Junctions* and *Foodpaths* events and this *Cookbook*, respectively. They proved themselves true collaborators and good friends. Thanks to Lesley Acton, Regan Koch, Hilary Jackson, Michael Kieber, Michael Stuart and Lucy Natarajan for proofreading some of the articles, Sara Wingate Gray for teaching us much about copyright, Felix Gonzales, Stephanie Thieullent and Kim Walker for taking photos and videos of the events, Sion Whellens for printing advice and Johannes Klotz for taking the picture of us, printed on the back cover.

Deepest thanks to Kaori O'Connor for mentorship, support and encouragement – and who always knew that there would be a book. She spent a great deal of time editing, proofreading and giving us all sorts of professional guidance. She came to our rescue through her subtle knowledge and detailed attention with far more kindness than we deserved. Without her being on our side from the outset, this book would never have been completed.

From Marina: At UCL, I consider myself very lucky to be part of such a stimulating learning environment. I must single out a number of academic staff who set me on the right path. These include: Robert Biel, my PhD supervisor, for the concepts of commons, grassroots mobilisation, our relationship with nature and the power of food; Caren Levy for strategic action planning and institutionalisation; Yves Cabannes for food sovereignty and participatory budgeting; Matthew Gandy for urban theories; Michael Edwards for his pioneering work on university-community engagement; Jane Rendell for critical spatial practice and the notions of social sculpture and a living artist; Muki Haklay for co-production of knowledge; Kevin Morgan for politics of care; Tim Lang for food democracy and Robin Murray for social innovation. I would also like to thank Rita Valencia for showing me that politics and spirituality are equally important and her commitment to North/South solidarity. A big thank you goes to Geoffrey Shepherd for helping my English and more importantly for the idea that there is a communion in food. There are many who from behind the scenes have encouraged and supported me, and I would like to thank them all but also respect their preference for remaining anonymous. I wouldn't have been able to do any of the work I have been involved in without the continued love and support of my father and mother who taught me responsibility, dedication and humility. Thanks also to my grandmother for inspiring me since my childhood, and showing me that food and cooking are more than making a meal.

From Lukas: A big thank you goes to my family for their support in literally everything I do: Ruth, Leo and Pia Meusburger. Even though she does not want to be mentioned here, I am also grateful for Moriyamo Olusoga's good ideas and her not being shy about expressing her critical opinions. Without friends, doing something like this book would be equally impossible and – out of many – I would like to give special thanks to Michael Kieber and Pascal Grosskopff for, among other things, letting me sleep very little during the last *Food Junctions* weekend. Thanks also to supportive flatmates Joakim Ivarson and Joshua Eichler-Summers for proofreading and general cheering up and Marta Pyrzyk for giving out *Food Junctions* flyers in the UCL Quad even though she didn't really want to.

Finally, we would like to dedicate this *Cookbook* to everyone who cares about food. As an urban farmer once told us, our attentiveness to growing food is a way of understanding our humanity and something greater than ourselves. It is about celebrating together. If we till the land and dig the well very deep, we may find out that we all have the same origins. That we all share natural resources is important. We wish to thank everyone for keeping the water flowing, the food growing, the kitchen cooking and our journey continuing.

Picture credits

All photos and/or images shown in each contribution belong to the author except for the following credits:

Acknowledgements:
    credit to Marina Chang
Introduction:
    credit to Stephanie Thieullent and
    Kim Walker

An edible architecture (right column-bottom):
    credit to Paul Smoothy
Cautious, competent, confident:
    credit to Marina Chang
Eating cats:
    credit to Marina Chang
Education with pesto:
    credit to Anne Carter
Financialised food:
    credit to Ray Witlin/World Bank (p. 57) and Nathan Cooke (p. 58)
Foodcycling:
    credit to Kim Walker (p. 74)
Food sovereignty:
    credit to Graciela Romero Vasquez
Fruit carving:
    credit to Stephanie Thieullent (top) and Kim Walker (middle and bottom)
Global Generation change:
    credit to Stephanie Thieullent (photos)
Harvesting fruit in the city:
    credit to Jonathan Goldberg (top) and Jon Enoch (bottom)
Himalayan meals:
    credit to Ian Fitzpatrick
Hot stuff:
    credit to Marina Chang
Kilburn station planters:
    Jonathan Goldberg

Making universities into better neighbours:
    credit to Kim Walker
Milkshake exclusif:
    credit to Ben Ottewell
Poetry menu:
    credit to Poet in the City (logos)
Save the pookato:
    credit to Emily Carter (illustration)
Silkworms and mulberry:
    credit to Marina Chang
Spice Caravan:
    credit to Maya Glaser
Tasting wine:
    credit to Marina Chang (top) and Lukas Meusburger (bottom)
This is a performance after all:
    credit to Vipul Sangoi
Urban food and sustainable cities:
    credit to Marina Chang

Editors' photo:
    credit to Johannes Klotz
Inside gated-folder photos:
    credit to Marina Chang

Foreword: **The complex wonder of food**

I **Professor Michael Worton**

I UCL Vice-Provost (Academics and International)

In every country in the world and in every society, the sharing of food is a vital element of community life, whether it be in celebratory feasting, performing religious rituals, sharing the most meagre of repasts, talking about food, making it together, using leftovers in gastronomically exciting ways or using them to fertilise our gardens or whatever. Food is central to our lives, essential to our well being, and above all a provider of happiness and joy.

Yet while we all know a great deal about food (and we all know what we like and what we don't like!), there is much about food that we do not know and much to learn, especially in an intercultural context.

Just as food is infinitely variable, so are the ways in which it is produced, cooked, written and talked about, eaten, sacralised and commemorated. In Spring 2010 for two weeks at the end of April and early May, UCL participated in the Reveal Festival in London by creating a student-led event on the theme of *Food Junctions*. The aim of *Food Junctions* was to mobilise the creativity of students and staff at UCL to create a wide variety of events in which new kinds of audiences were brought together in order to think about food. In other words, *Food Junctions* was precisely that – a series of crossings, of explorations of the ideas of food for thought and food for the body, encouraging everyone who attended the very different events to understand better just how marvellously

complex food is in its existence, in the way it is created, and in the way that it is used.

Food Junctions brought together people from many different disciplines and cultures, with one of the main aims being the creation not only of better understanding of food, but also better connectedness between communities and within communities.

The events which took place across many venues in Camden were a terrific success. At the end, there was a great sense of achievement and delight in the many new (and lasting) friendships that had grown out of meetings when engaging in gardening or trying out different ways of baking or listening to or reciting poetry or tasting wine or simply enthusing together about 'food, glorious food!'. The founding group therefore decided that the following year they would do more, and throughout the first few months of 2011, they launched a new project, *Foodpaths*, creating a series of events to engage yet more people. Again, a host of events were organised, including learning about organisations which provide hot free meals every week for vulnerable people; about innovative food growing initiatives and about new kinds of cafés run as social enterprises. There were meetings where everyone was asked to bring a herb or spice and to share what it meant with the others, and events which involved working with catering co-ops of refugee women bringing their cuisines to audiences which didn't know them. Issues of food security were discussed, as were ways of how best to grow food in London. There were events ranging from 'food and women' to 'food and co-operatives', from 'food and oral health' to 'food and spirituality'.

It became clear that the *Food Junctions* idea, created for a particular festival initiated by Create KX, the advocacy group from Kings Cross, was something that had grown organically and also absolutely had to continue. Very often, we talk about the importance of sustainability when we undertake initiatives. In this case, the sustainability of the *Food Junctions* project was assured almost from the very start by the enthusiasm and the commitment of the core group. Of course there were - and will continue to be - challenges in maintaining the project, but the ways in which many thousands of people have been affected, informed and above all enthused and delighted by the *Food Junctions* initiative is what will guarantee, I am sure, its future.

Part of this future and part of its sustainability is this *Cookbook*. True to their all-embracing, holistic view of food, the editors of the *Cookbook* have taken both a literal and a metaphorical view of the term '*Cookbook*', and you will find in this volume many contributions which will make you rethink not only what 'cooking' and 'food' are, but also what a 'book' is. Because this is not just a book. It is an eye-opener, a mind-expander,

a thought-provoker, and above all a joy – in the way that it will make you think and live and eat and cook and sing and dance and feel better in the world.

As Vice-Provost of UCL, I am enormously proud of the work of the editors and of everyone involved in *Food Junctions* and *Foodpaths* over the past two years. It has been both inspiring and humbling to follow their progress as they engage so many people in so many different ways of thinking about one of the most basic elements of every human being's life. The *Food Junctions Cookbook* is another example of their innovative approach to thinking and being.

This is a book to read quickly and to read slowly, a book to savour and to relish; a book to return to time and again when you need cheering and inspiration.

Read it!

Introduction

I **Marina Chang**

I Development Planning Unit, UCL

Before reading this small book, please look at the cover for a few minutes. What do you see? A group of people having a meal together, or do trees full of apples first catch your attention? Then, perhaps, you notice a farm house with a cow and two farmers working in the field. You might look downwards and see a globe: on it is a woman with a food basket on her head and a man eating an apple with his digestive system clearly showing. On the left, you might discover a fish swimming, a honey bee and a butterfly. Wait a second, you eagerly say, 'I can also see two unusual street signs, with a tricycle in front and vegetable shops and buildings in the background.' It is only at this moment that you notice the title of the book - *The Food Junctions Cookbook: Living Recipes for Social Innovation* - and you feel puzzled and ask yourself what sort of cookbook it might be and what is meant by the words 'living recipes for social innovation.'

In the spring of 2009, as a part of coursework, I produced a huge table-cloth to communicate the significance of food and its relationship with the world we live in. In this view of food and its meaning, the kitchen is the pivotal point. It is a place where we share meals, exchange ideas, engage with the world. That particular table-cloth contains many texts and images relating to food and agriculture. I decided to name this work - *A Living Kitchen: New Aesthetics of Food* - suggesting that a kitchen is a 'living organism'. That was a first attempt to bring people from different backgrounds and cultures together, to create a new kind of community and to point to the idea that everything connects.

This table-cloth has been well used on many different occasions over the last two years in many places, especially in community gardens in London. The table-cloth has become an icon for us at *Food Junctions* and *Foodpaths* - the names we gave to our two major food projects. Those taking part in the events were invited to work out the visible patterns and invisible connections that were displayed on or suggested by the table-cloth. At times, they picked up fresh vegetables directly from the garden, and washed, cooked and ate them together around the table-cloth, while discussing their ideas about food. This table-cloth now carries traces of food we have harvested, cooked and eaten. The colour has become faded after many washes but the memory of sharing still remains. So when we started to think of a fitting design for the book-cover, there was an immediate response that we should continue to use the design of the table-cloth.

We know, for sure, that you all have different views and ideas, so there might be no consensus over the meanings and feelings expressed on the cover design. Here, we just offer you one way to look at it from our perspective. The pictures show relationships between living individuals and their environment. On the one hand, our aim is to bring together the concept of life in the country and cities and the meeting of nature and culture. We envisage a 'zero waste' society and lifestyle where natural resources are better managed and regenerated. Specifically, in food and agriculture systems, we suggest a shorter food supply chain; for example, our food waste from the kitchen and dining table becomes organic composting fertiliser and food for livestock. The other aim is to bring people of all sorts into the unity of a shared meal around the table-cloth, where taking food and drink together creates the spirit of love and friendship. The two street signs drawn from the logos of *Food Junctions* and *Foodpaths* can also be seen as indicating a way forward towards our two aims.

In putting forward these aims, we were inspired by the belief of Joseph Beuys that every human being is a living artist who can see, think and reshape his or her life actively. However, while we appreciated this vision, we also hoped to extend the call for creativity, imagination

and innovation and develop it on a larger scale. The notion of 'social innovation' seemed to serve our purpose. The term 'social innovation' is an emerging and evolving concept. We find its key idea of 'connected difference', whether a new combination of existing elements or a cutting across boundaries, very compelling. There are at least four interrelated themes to be considered in our understanding of social innovation. Firstly, the theory and philosophy of social change, whether as minor-key alternatives or radical revolution, whether at local or broader levels; secondly, the experience of living the change in our everyday life; thirdly, the process involved in the making of social change; and lastly, the outcome of such experiments.

We embraced different definitions of social innovation at *Food Junctions* and *Foodpaths* according to their particular contexts. At *Food Junctions*, we emphasised that cities have a remarkable capacity for generating a tremendous

range of social relations and new ways of living with or among others. In the festival we organised, we elaborated on the idea that a festival is an intensified celebration of everyday life where we can explore how diverse forms of food, agricultural knowledge and practices are addressed, assembled and enhanced. Festivals are usually funny and entertaining events where people don't expect provocation; this one was different. *Food Junctions* was an edible experiment, a new way of slotting in some ideas that people do not usually think about, and helping people to react to those ideas, whether they were political, economic or social. The fact that we worked closely with our hosts Camley Street Natural Park, part of the London Wildlife Trust, also reflected our vision of engaging London's diverse communities, both human and non-human, with nature in the built environment.

As a continuation of *Food Junctions*, we hoped to go a bit further at *Foodpaths*. It was a strategic decision to focus on the King's Cross area as UCL is part of the King's Cross community. Large scale regeneration is happening within the King's Cross area and the transitional stage is also a window of opportunity to work out possible new paths, including practical methods and support for more sustainable food networks at the local level. We organised our events at the Calthorpe Project, a community kitchen within a community garden in the heart of King's Cross. We called it '*Foodpaths: the King's Cross Movement*' because

we wanted to highlight the role of the university in facilitating knowledge-exchange and experience-sharing through and for the urban food movement. We were also keen to explore how a university like UCL can work with and help the local communities, particularly those more marginalised groups of the population.

In the course of editing this book, we came to realise that learning from nature is an important factor in developing the notion of 'social innovation'. For example, the ways animals act communally. Bees act collectively for the benefit of the group and keep the hive intact. Other ways of life in the natural world are equally important and examples can be found in the lives of birds, earthworms and trees, to name just a few. While birds fly high and survey broad vistas of the landscape, earthworms live in the mud below, but they help us by fertilising the barren soil, which is central to the growth of food. Trees in their complex systems not only give us shade and comfort, but with their size and strength have the capacity to shelter many different living species. More importantly, their root systems bind and water the soil around them. Trees draw life into their systems and also give life in return.

With our definition of social innovation, we can now introduce what we mean by 'living recipes'. The word 'recipe' is of course a food recipe but in this context it also means a way of living, which in turn can be divided into three parts: biological and ecological; social and political; and cultural and spiritual. It is the diversity of our contributors in this Cookbook and their values and ideas that make these recipes 'live' through personal stories and recipes.

This Cookbook represents our commitment to collaborative endeavour on several levels. It definitely represents collaboration among the core team members. It all started from a few meals together; we shared our frustration that we as students often felt our studies did not directly impact on society and our yearning to actually do something transformative, however modest it might be. Throughout Food Junctions, Foodpaths and now the Cookbook, the level of passion, enthusiasm and dedication among the core team members was just incredible. We were most critical with one another but always in a cooperative and constructive manner, striving for excellence. We made decisions through long deliberative conversations but also respected and trusted in each person's strength and professionalism to make the best judgement on their own. We like to call ourselves cooks in that we 'cook' our projects together. While it is said that 'too many cooks spoil the broth', our case contradicts this, and instead proves that 'many hands make light work'.

The Cookbook is also a kind of multidisciplinary collaboration. Given the evident complexity in our food and agricultural systems, we insisted on the need to think and work in a multidisciplinary fashion. We tried to create an inclusive platform to accommodate the 'fields of possibilities' and remove unwanted bias within specific disciplines. Moreover, this *Cookbook* is a collaboration between university and communities. Food is something everyone experiences, and can identify with and understand. We are grateful that we have been given so much support from the university to help us to engage with communities through a common interest in food in our everyday life. The past few years have seen a growing recognition that work on food and agriculture in communities is a uniquely valuable way of addressing many vital issues. Incorporating contributions from these two groups of people brings new insights into our integrative understanding of food, agriculture and society, both locally and globally. Finally, the *Cookbook* is a collaboration between us and many friends, colleagues, and family members as well as a number of people who wanted to contribute an article but, for whatever reasons, couldn't make it. In spite of this, they have given us their support and of course lovely meals. Their roles in the creation of this *Cookbook* cannot be ignored.

Most of our contributors had some involvement at *Food Junctions* and *Food-*

We are collective cooks at *Food Junctions*.

paths, whether as organisers, speakers, partners, volunteers, or participants. Half of our contributors are from universities, mainly from UCL but with a small number from other universities both in London and elsewhere. The other half of the contributors are from the community, both groups and individuals. We have welcomed people from all walks of life. It has been a long and difficult journey. Many meetings, conversations and email communications took place between editors, proof-readers and our contributors as well as physical journeys, mostly on foot, between the university campus and numerous community centres in London. It is interesting to see that the subject of food has been increasingly discussed in the media and in politics on a national level, and that a much higher proportion of the contributors now talk about growing food in the city, demonstrating that this is a hot topic in London.

Because of this, the *Cookbook* is timely in its production. We have developed a better understanding of our relationship with food, here in London as well as in the rest of the world. We hope to respond to certain political and ideological debates such as food security and food sovereignty by exploring challenges that confront us and the possible pathways we can take in the twenty-first century. We like to believe that we are in a stronger position to fulfil what was stated in our original bid for the funding of *Food Junctions*, in which we said that 'we want to tell our stories, as

students within particular departments and across the UCL community; as local residents around King's Cross and as global citizens. It may all start from tending an apple tree, taking a guided walk, or cooking a meal together and chatting around a kitchen table.'

Like many Taiwanese, I have a flexible and spontaneous approach to using recipes. My mother and grandmother used to tell me things like 'put in a little bit of this or that' and 'for a few minutes' without precise measurements of weight and time. By no means am I suggesting that this is the best way to learn a new recipe. However, what makes this worth sharing is the freedom it gives you to be 'inspired' by a recipe, to follow your preferences and to use what you have available. In this way, you actively engage with and create what you desire, and make the best use you can of what there is. It is a bodily practice that uses your brain and senses, and above all your heart to judge the right balance between ingredients. All we want to say is that, instead of simply believing or following what is presented here in the *Cookbook*, pick up some 'recipes' which interest you the most and try them out. The idea of 'living recipes' will never be 'living' enough, unless you are cooking them, either on your own or together with others in your home and communities. In so doing, you actually make this *Cookbook* a genuine collaboration.

5-A-GREEN

| Sandhya Kaffo
| FOODDOTS

"Everyone thinks of changing the world, but no one thinks of changing himself" Leo Tolstoy, the Russian mystic and novelist, once said.

This quote couldn't be more apt than in these current times. Everyone is trying to save the planet but not many are trying to save their own bodies which are equally deteriorating.

Everyone is promoting one green initiative or another but not many are driving initiatives to cut to the core of sustainable health and longevity. The green 'evolution' is rampant but the green 'involution' does not even appear on the radar. In order to create balance, the other side of the scale also needs to be ramped up.

Every step along the food chain, from soil to table, we vote with our purses by the food choices we make. Every step of the way, no matter how we justify it, we make a significant impact on both the planetary body and the physical body.

Our foods have increasingly diverged from nature's foodpath of wholesome, nutrient-dense and life-giving foods to an industrialised system of processed, preserved, packaged and under-nourishing foods. 'As within so without', our bodies have equally taken a u-turn from

health to the 'dead man walking' syndrome. Dead food makes dead people. The unhealthy state of the human form and its decline is staggering and the sad part of it all is that it is becoming the norm to be diseased.

I feel strongly that it is the right of the human body to be nourished on every level and to be stupendously healthy and it is our individual responsibility to effect the change from the inside out. Only with this mindset will there be balance and harmony between the planetary body and the physical body.

I have looked far and wide and each time I see what lands on our food plates, the root cause of our deteriorating state of well-being becomes obvious. There is a tremendous lack of colourful, fresh and vibrant plant based foods in adequate quantities to make a difference. The king of all foods – fresh, vibrant and leafy dark greens – are given no thought at all or perched on the side of the plate as an afterthought.

5 A DAY does not even begin to scratch the surface as a solution to this most glaring problem and were I to run a similar campaign of this magnitude it would be for a 5-A-GREEN to begin to make a real difference and I know it will. If you're going to advocate Green Living to the extent we're purporting, then it is imperative that we start with Green Eating. Green Eating goes beyond the greens on a plate but respects the whole process of nature's food chain

leading to a more conscious way of shopping, eating and living. Conscious eating is conscious living.

Recipe for conscious eating in 5 easily digestible chunks:

1. Add at least 50% fresh leafy greens, wild greens and fresh herbs to daily meals. Leafy greens are potent medicinal foods, full of life force and nutrient-dense and are best eaten fresh and uncooked. They contain chlorophyll which not only nourishes the blood but is also the quickest way to keep the body in alkaline balance.

2. Grow a herb in a small pot to begin to connect to nature's growing process. Gardeners we may not all be but much can be achieved by just growing one pot of something. The fact that all you need is a pot, soil and a seed to grow amazing food is testament to the simplicity that nature chooses to feed us well.

3. Shop at your local farmers' market, get to know where your food comes from, and cherish the quality of food rather than focusing on the quantity.

4. Learn the life skill of preparing fresh meals while nourishing your body through the process. You have only lasting sustainable energy and health to gain and the waste of ingesting junk food to lose.

5. Nourish your body as you would the planet. Save yourself first, in order to save the planet. If we understand that what we choose to eat we choose to become, then we choose what we become through our food choices.

A 5-A-GREEN smoothie recipe:
For a balanced world of planetary and physical health.

Ingredients:
Spinach leaves - 1 handful
Parsley herbs - 2 fingertips
Green apple - 1 cored small apple
Lime - juice of a quarter of a lime
Avocado - peel and core half a ripe avocado
Water - add a cup of water

To make:
Blend till very smooth
Drink with joy and pleasure.

Allotment soups

I Dr. Robert Biel
I Development Planning Unit, UCL

I am including two soup recipes; nettle and run-to-seed cabbages, which respectively emphasise, firstly, the need to harmonise with nature, and secondly, the approach to socio-institutional development.

Nettle can be considered the basic ingredient of the first soup, which emphasises the recipe's relationship to foraged natural food: it is rich in minerals, oligo-elements etc. Sorrel is a perennial plant which is close to a wild form. Because it is perennial it fits in well with low-impact food growing, which should generally seek to counter excessive emphasis on annuals. It imparts a richness of flavour, while buckwheat leaves are extremely rich in antioxidants. Buckwheat also illustrates another aspect of low-impact gardening: in addition to using really wild plants like nettle we are also mimicking nature; buckwheat is typically used as a green manure which imitates the way wild plants would quickly establish themselves on any denuded portion of land, and thus maintain soil structure and prevent leaching of nutrients; but the green manures should also be multi-use, i.e. we can eat them and not just plough them in. The potato, whose function is to bind the soup and improve the consistency, could be a first early variety such as Red Duke of York, in order to coincide with the later harvests of nettles. The soup is extremely healthy because of the balanced combination of different ingredients. People generally say "you can feel it doing you good" ... which may be partly because of the euphoriant effect of the serotonin which nettles also contain!

Nettle soup:

Ingredients:
Tips of nettles
Sorrel leaves (equal quantity to nettles)
Buckwheat leaves
1 potato
Lemon juice
Red chilli
Light soy sauce
Black pepper

To make:
Combine all ingredients (except lemon juice and black pepper), cover with water and simmer; it helps to simmer for some time, about 1 hour. Then purée and add lemon juice and black pepper (possibly also salt, but light soy sauce generally makes it salty enough) to taste.

Run-to-seed cabbages make up the main ingredient of the second recipe. One reason to include the recipe was to emphasise how we must escape the waste and homogenisation imposed by the supermarket system. Currently it would be difficult to commercialise a cabbage which has developed in a chaotic way by following its inclination to flower, but from a culinary point of view this may well be when it is at its best. But the main reason is that I learned it from the group Reclaim our Food in Brixton, South London. They represent the more radical trend of the environmental movement, which has met with significant repression (e.g. see http://tinyurl.com/reclaimingfood). In order to escape the catastrophe of the current food system (and of the current system more generally) we need a radical realignment or self-organisation of the different elements of society. At present there are many experiments in local and community food production, but the risk is that they be hijacked by a neo-liberal discourse masquerading under the guise of community empowerment, in which case all the potential for change would be lost. This is why we must affirm the radical fringe which is less in thrall to the current alignment.

Run-to-seed cabbage soup:

Ingredients:
Cabbages - which have been allowed to run to seed but are still tender
Onion
Curry powder
Coconut cream
Seasoning to taste

To make:
Sauté curry powder in a little oil to develop the aroma; slice and add onion and continue frying; roughly chop run-to-seed cabbage and add to the pan; grate coconut cream, add to pan and stir; add water, cook for about half an hour, purée and serve.

An edible architecture

| Richard Beckett

I The Bartlett, Faculty of the Built Environment, UCL

It was the discovery of a cottage built of ginger-bread and cakes with window panes of clear sugar that almost led to the demise of Hansel and Gretel as depicted by the Brothers Grimm.

How were they to know that in fact the hostess of this most delicious of houses was indeed a 'wicked witch' whose sole aim was to waylay the hungry children with the intent of cooking and eating them? How were they to also know that said wicked witch's house was probably in serious breach of planning laws and no doubt of very poor structural integrity? One call to the local council could have put an earlier stop to the witch's evil conniving, or at least forced her to rebuild the house with materials more structurally suitable than gingerbread - materials ultimately less alluring to hungry children.

Overlooking such pedantry, the relationships between food and architecture were manifest long before the scheming of the wicked witch. The foundations of culture and the beginnings of civilisations emerged together with our primal needs for food and shelter. Finding and preparing a place in the earth for growing food meant the development of permanent shelter was needed. In more recent history, food and architecture

have typically been associated with celebration, particularly after war to demonstrate power, wealth and abundance, or to celebrate the life of a king or saint. Indeed the Arch of Vigilance, constructed to celebrate St. John the Baptist's Day in Italy in 1629, was literally constructed of cheese, ham, sausages, and roast piglets. Even in the simplest terms, the conversion of basic raw ingredients into a fine meal can be compared similarly to the transformation of raw building materials into designed architecture.

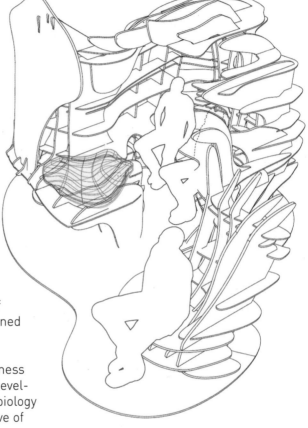

In a time of ecological consciousness and sustainable futures, recent developments in genetics, molecular biology and biochemistry now offer a wave of new possibilities in relation to the way we produce and eat food, and also allows consideration of a new architecture that is sophisticated through its use of novel materials. A new wave of experiments are being undertaken that utilise living or biological materials, many of which are derived from food crops, to create an architecture that is a semi-living entity that can become a symbiotic part of an existing ecology.

The idea that one could grow parts of buildings, or allow other areas to bio-degrade depending on the user's needs is a provocative concept. Buildings are never really permanent – even concrete

degrades – but it is the way in which our building materials decompose that could be considered as more important with regard to our ecosystems. Plastics in particular are a major problem to our ecosystems in that together with taking hundreds of years to degrade, some also release pollutants during the degradation process.

Biopolymers which display the same properties as conventional oil-based plastics can now be derived from corn crops to produce a material that has many applications. Such a material will biodegrade safely on compost heaps or in water systems when no longer needed. Molecular and genetic manipulation will allow us to control for how long such materials can be used before they begin to degrade.

The Food Junction Folly was an experimental installation project developed for a *Food Junctions* event which followed previous NURBSTER constructions done by marcosandmarjan in which the ma-

terial efficiency of CAD-operated 2D and 3D design processes were explored with the use of sophisticated computer numerically controlled (CNC) techniques. Such work did not just aim for an efficient and optimised way of managing material and time, it also expressed the functional as well as deliberately ornamental character of the construction techniques of cut-joint fittings without additional fixings for quick assembly and disassembly.

The folly was designed around the social acts of discussion and collaboration, with space for two or three people to sit, discuss and share recipes and cooking ideas. As an experiment in a semi-living architecture, parts of the folly were constructed using a biodegradable corn based biopolymer. Throughout the event these surfaces were used as integrated parts of the installation – a table surface to share recipes and a softer part of the bench surface to sit on. After the event, however, these parts of the installation become more and more a part of the ecology of the site. As the parts begin to biodegrade the architecture starts to become part of the food chain, not necessar-

ily for the users but certainly for birds, insects and other microbial organisms already present on the site. The use of such a material produces an architec-

Edible lego bricks:

Ingredients:
4 tbsp cornflour
20g gelatin
500ml water
1 tsp glycerine
1 tsp vinegar

To make:
Mix the cornflour, gelatin and water together over a medium heat. Add the glycerine and vinegar and stir well. Divide the liquid in to 4 lots, add different food colourings to each lot then pour into an ice cube tray and allow to set in a warm place - edible lego blocks.

Not particularly tasty to you and me perhaps but once you have finished playing at building, throw them on the compost or the bottom of the garden to provide nutrients for your soil, birds and insects.

ture that is anthropocentric in its design but ecocentric in its lifespan. An edible architecture which, granted, is not quite as delicious as the gingerbread and cakes of the wicked witch's house, but it is certainly more structurally sound and not a single child was cooked or eaten during the process.

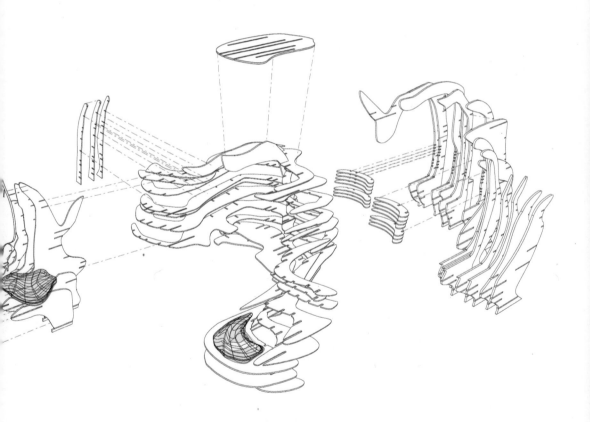

Baghali polo makes me happy

I **Minoosh Seifi**

Baghali polo is a Persian dish which goes back hundreds of years.

Polo in Persian means steamed rice. To make *Baghali polo* for one person, soak a cup of rice in cold water, add a pinch of salt, then bring to boil until the rice is still firm. Drain the rice and rinse it with cold water (this will help to let out the starch). Add 3 tablespoons of either fresh finely chopped dill or dried, ¼ teaspoon of saffron brewed in a little water for ten minutes, a little salt, and pre-cooked broad beans to the rice. Allow the rice mixture to steam in a non-stick saucepan until the rice becomes fluffy. The lid of the pan should be wrapped in a cloth to prevent the steam from escaping. You can sprinkle a tablespoon of sunflower oil, olive oil or sesame seed oil on the rice after you have taken it off the heat to steam a little more on a lower temperature.

The natural and colourful ingredients used in the dish are responsible for its famous presence at times of happiness and celebration in Persian culture. The green colour of broad beans gives the rice a fresh feel that is associated with happiness and luck in Persian culture. The warm orange-yellow colour of Persian saffron and its aroma make one smile. The deep green colour of the dill and its aromatic taste reminds us of the goodness that nature has given us. My grandmother, who loved cooking and inviting people around for lunch or dinner used to tell us that making this dish made her happy because everyone around the *sofreh*[1] was always smiling. If you are a meat lover you can have this dish with chicken or lamb cooked in saffron. If you are vegan or vegetarian, yogurt and salads go very well with *Baghali polo*.

I decided to write about this dish, as it is a nutritious food for all. No matter whether you are a meat lover, vegetarian or vegan, you can have this dish either with or without meat together with the side dishes recommended above. I moved to the UK when I was very young. Initially, I could not cook at all. I used to buy a lot of processed food from supermarkets. However, after a year I felt very unhealthy. So I became determined to improve my eating habits. I observed my Japanese, Chinese, Korean and other friends from different cultures and asked my mother how I could cook the dishes that she used to make me when I lived at home. When she gives me a recipe for a dish, I often improvise using my creativity and the methods used by my international friends. I was very pleased with the first dish I made and gained encouragement to cook for my friends who have so far enjoyed my dishes. I have continuously tried to make healthier food by using natural ingredients, gaining inspiration

---

[1] In Persian, traditionally, a long specially-made cloth called *sofreh* is spread on a Persian handmade carpet so that people can sit around it and eat. The food is placed in the centre in big dishes so that people can help themselves to as much food as they like.

from other cultures and using more efficient methods when cooking. For me, the secret is mixing natural ingredients that go together, using herbs and experimenting with spices from different countries. Natural food makes me happier and healthier while connecting me with people from different cultures with similar aspirations. It also allows me to be more environmentally friendly by using home-grown or locally grown vegetables and herbs.

Banana bread

I **Dr. Kaori O'Connor**
I Department of Anthropology, UCL

The Pacific islands of Hawaii – the most isolated inhabited place · on earth – have always drawn migrants who brought their foods with them.

The first Polynesian voyagers brought taro, sweet potato, coconut and some twenty-four different types of bananas, which along with pigs cooked in earth ovens were the key foods in the famed Hawaiian feasts known as *'luaus'*. Subsequent waves of immigration came from East and Southeast Asia, Europe, North America and the South Pacific, resulting over several generations in a cosmopolitan population, and in a multicultural cuisine that is often served up in the distinctive island form known as 'plate lunches'. Bewildering to visitors and irresistible to islanders, these meals sold from mobile lunch wagons, lunch stands or in 'local' style cafés consist of scoops of rice and macaroni salad, partnered with two, three or more items from a selection of local favourites that includes chicken curry, pineapple spare ribs, Hawaiian style pork, Korean barbecue, short rib stew, fried mahimahi fish and much more, mixtures islanders became accustomed to through generations of sharing each other's foods at work and play. This is history you can eat – the original Hawaiian cuisine overlaid layer upon layer with the foods of later migrants, who came to work during Hawaii's plantation era, long before tourism began. Yet just as history can be read from plates, so it is inscribed on bodies.

Of all 'local' dishes, banana bread is one of the best-loved. The deep Hawaiian valleys were planted with banana trees, which produced great golden 'hands' of luscious fruit, a favourite use for which was to make banana bread. This brown and buttery loaf cake sweetened with island cane sugar seemed to have always been part of the Hawaiian culinary repertoire, for every island family had its own recipe, and it wasn't for many years that the perils as well as the pleasures of imported foodways became apparent. Banana bread, it is now clear, is a paradigm example of culinary and environmental colonialism, and of the bittersweet aftertaste of sugar.

The American Congregationalist missionaries who came to the islands in 1820 had a dual objective: religious and cultural conversion. As part of what they saw as their 'civilising mission', they stopped the islanders from eating their native foods in raw or simply prepared form as was customary, and obliged them to cook and eat in a western manner, introducing them to the bread and cake cuisine of New England, which the missionaries considered foods of refinement and sanctity. As in the Caribbean, the world's growing taste for sweetness caused much of the Hawaiian Islands to be planted in sugar cane, introducing the economic instability that comes with relying on only one or two crops, destroying the diversity of the local ecosystem and making the population dependent on imported tinned and processed foods.

This shift in diet along with an increasingly sedentary lifestyle resulted in Polynesian people now having the highest rates of obesity and diabetes in the world, which a local community doctor, Terry Shintani, managed to treat by having his Polynesian patients return to eating fresh, unrefined foods as their ancestors had – raw bananas instead of banana bread, baked taro instead of taro bread, coconuts instead of coconut cake. This regime was so successful that, adapted for general use, it featured on the American best-seller list under the title *The Hawaii Diet*. Yet even this book had a recipe for banana bread, so central is it to Hawaiian culture and cuisine today.

Here is my family recipe. I hope you will enjoy it, although not too often, and even if you never cook it, that it will have taught you something about the histories hidden on plates and in recipes.

'Hawaiian' banana bread:

Ingredients (American measurements):

2 cups plain flour
1 cup caster sugar
1/2 cup butter
2 eggs
5 ripe bananas
1/2 cup chopped walnuts or macadamia nuts
1 tsp baking soda
1 tsp salt

To make:

Cream together sugar and butter. Add beaten eggs and mashed ripe bananas. Sift together baking soda, salt and plain flour. Add to banana mixture, stirring well but not too long. Add chopped walnuts or macadamia nuts. Bake in two medium loaf pans, well greased, in a preheated 325-350°F (160-180°C) oven for one hour.

A bannock-eye view of history

I **Laura Ishiguro**

I Department of History, UCL

No dish encapsulates Canada's history of cultural encounter, colonialism and multiculturalism better than bannock.

Also known as frybread, bannock is a quick bread that developed from the intersections of indigenous and Scottish food traditions during the fur trade era. Over the past three centuries, different groups of people in Canada have shared, consumed, adapted and regulated the dish as they navigated changing relationships with one another.

Before contact with Europeans, many indigenous groups in North America made quick breads using roots, tree sap, cornmeal and other plant products. In the eighteenth century, Scottish explorers and fur traders spread across the continent, bringing with them another kind of bread, which they called bannock. The fur trade was characterised by extensive cultural exchange between indigenous and non-indigenous people. Out of this context grew a new bread, named for the Scottish bannock and combining cultural traditions while adapting to local conditions.

For European traders and indigenous communities, who were constantly mobile during this period, this was a useful dish because it required few ingredients and very little cooking equipment. It used European ingredients like flour and, by the nineteenth century, leaveners like baking soda and baking powder. These preserved well and the other main ingredient, water, was easy to acquire in the backwoods. The dish itself was usually cooked on a cast-iron frying pan over a fire.

Bannock continued to grow in popularity in the nineteenth century with the development of rural industries such as logging and mining. Often accompanied by beans or bacon, it was a quick and simple recipe that was easily mastered in rural campsites, even by new arrivals unaccustomed to cooking for themselves.

Bannock:

Ingredients:
300g flour
2 tsp baking powder
Pinch of salt
Approximately 250ml cold water
Oil (or lard, butter or bacon grease)

To make:
Heat about 1 cm of oil in a frying pan at medium-high heat. In a bowl, mix dry ingredients, then make a well in the centre. Add water and mix; you want a dough that is relatively thick and firm. Divide into about five small cakes and flatten to 2 cm thick. Fry in oil, and shake to prevent sticking. Flip when golden brown crust forms on the bottom side. Takes about 8-10 minutes to brown on both sides. Can also be baked (180° C, approximately 15 minutes) or even cooked on a stick over a fire until golden brown (see picture).

The dish became popular precisely because of its flexibility, so play around with the recipe. Eat with stew or soup; mix dried fruit or seeds into the dough; top with honey, powdered sugar, cinnamon, maple syrup or brown sugar; or serve with strawberries and whipped cream. Use your imagination and give it your own flavour!

However, the history of bannock is not just one of cultural adaptation and exchange. By the end of the nineteenth century, indigenous communities across Canada had lost access to traditional lands and resources as the government delineated small reserves for them and opened up the rest of the territory to non-indigenous settlers.

Government agents supplied reserve communities with rations of flour as part of treaty obligations or in response to petitions. Bannock, reliant on flour, thus became further incorporated into indigenous diets. At the same time, the Department of Indian Affairs also sought to regulate and control every aspect of indigenous lives as part of a 'civilising mission.' In the process, the government even banned bannock in 1889; cooked over a fire and requiring little equipment, the dish seemed to represent and enable the nomadic, seasonal lifestyle that they sought to eliminate.

Bannock did not disappear under the ban. Today it is eaten at community celebrations like powwows, as well as at family dinners and hikers' campsites across the country. Modern bannock is neither the Scottish nor the indigenous quick breads of the eighteenth century, but rather has developed over time in relation to changing ingredients, cooking conditions and forms of cultural encounter from fur trade cooperation, to colonial regulation, to modern celebrations of multiculturalism.

Catherine's cherry kisses

| Karen Rumsey

| Division of Infection & Immunity, UCL

King Charles II's wife Catherine of Braganza is credited with making the drinking of tea fashionable in England. Here they share an afternoon tea.

He stretched out his languorous legs, settled into the hillock of cushions and, waving away the maid servant, snorted: "Lely's picture makes you look like a ..." "Mistress, perhaps, Your Majesty." He was silenced, briefly; as in fact, was I; we neither of us wishing to break the possibility of harmony.

Love and scandal are the best sweeteners of tea.
Henry Fielding, "Love in Several Masques"

"True beauty," he countered and plunged his fork into the delicate choux pastrywork positioned coquettishly on the richly painted tea plate. The fork's girth was half that of his index finger, he struggled to wield control of the tiny yet exquisitely crafted silver tool and the resultant crash of silver and china clattered around the room. I watched a look of annoyance cross his face and then he looked up and so did I and we both giggled. He picked up the miscreant piece of pastry on his fork and placing his other hand under the sugar-packed load, directed it into my mouth and stroked my cheek.

"This is the best of our Indies," he observed as he looked into his tea, the steam having given way to a smooth sandy surface that he broke with a gulp. He always enjoyed the smack of nearly scalding tea on his throat while I preferred mine as a cooling liquid that could be sipped and considered. "The best of the Indies for the best of the day?" I suggested. He smiled and his raven eyes softened, "Indeed, my love, indeed." In the near silence of our daily ritual we played and replayed our own private understanding: a love measured out in cups of tea.

Cherry kisses:
Makes 9 or 10 individual kisses

Ingredients:
4oz butter
4oz caster sugar (or fruit sugar – use a little less)
4oz self raising flour
2 eggs, beaten
1 tbsp cocoa powder
Red jam (cherry, raspberry, strawberry)
20 glace cherries (for inside and topping)
3 tbsp icing sugar

To make:

1. Pre-heat oven to 180°C.
2. Cream butter into a smooth paste; add caster sugar and beat until smooth.
3. Sift self-raising flour with cocoa powder.
4. Add beaten eggs and flour/cocoa powder into creamed butter and sugar; add a little water/milk if the mixture becomes dry.
5. In each cake case, place 2 tsp cake mixture in the base, add 1 tsp jam and a glace cherry, and cover this with 1 or 2 tsp cake mixture.
6. Place the cakes in the centre of the oven and bake for 25 minutes (when cooked the cake mixture should be firm to the touch).
7. The topping: cream butter and add 3 tbsp icing sugar sifted with 1 tbsp cocoa and then 1 or 2 tsp of hot water. Beat the mixture into a creamy slightly stiff mixture.
8. When the cakes are cool, use a knife to lavishly coat/smooth the topping over the cakes.
9. Add another cherry to the top and dust with icing sugar or cake glitter.
10. Mwah!

Cautious, competent, confident

| Samantha Bilton

If you are reading this article then there is a good chance you enjoy cooking. But what sort of a cook are you? Do you follow a recipe religiously or do you use cookbooks for inspiration to concoct your own culinary creations?

I conducted some research at the University of Brighton to discover how cookbooks influence the domestic cook. The findings of this research project indicated the type of cookbook or writer preferred is dependent on the confidence level of the cook. Cautious cooks have the least confidence (although not necessarily less skill) and prefer step by step guides with pictures. They are more likely to follow a recipe to the letter and to stick to a tried and tested author such as Delia Smith. Competent cooks take an *ad hoc* approach to every-day cooking but will refer to a recipe when entertaining friends. On the whole these cooks prefer quick and easy recipes such as those produced by Jamie Oliver. Finally, confident cooks have the most self-assurance in the kitchen and are more likely to use cookbooks for inspiration rather than instruction. They rely on their instinct and are happy to experiment with ingredients to make a recipe their own. They are the most likely to use a recipe without

a picture and prefer authors who give them free reign to experiment such as Nigel Slater. It was interesting to hear that even confident cooks could become cautious cooks depending on whom they were cooking for.

Cooking is a task that most of us undertake at some point during the day even if that only extends to heating up a ready meal in the microwave. However, high sales of cookbooks and the proliferation of television cookery programmes indicate that the British have a great interest in cooking to the point where cooking at home has been elevated to an art form. Conversely, the decline in our nation's ability to cook from scratch has been publically lamented by culinary paragons such as Prue Leith. It has been argued that the advent of convenience foods has freed up women's time which allows them to work outside of the home more. As a result children are not witnessing their mothers cooking from scratch and skills are not being passed on. A further argument for the deskilling of home cooks is that it is a direct result of home economics being removed from the national curriculum. The supermarkets have also done a fantastic job of providing us with all the ingredients we need to prepare a meal quickly without actually having to get our hands dirty. Why waste valuable time cooking when it could be spent watching someone far more competent doing it on television? The research highlighted that for many people the thought of cooking is intimidating. This fear is fuelled by programmes like Masterchef that raise domestic cooking to a professional level. These cautious cooks fear failure and disappointment and are reluctant to participate. The reticence to cook will remain as long as people believe it is a complex and longwinded activity. The key to building culinary confidence is not to put pressure on those people who never cook or who are fearful of cooking to become expert amateur chefs. Cooking does not have to be as complicated as some cookbooks or television programmes portray it. Nor does it necessarily have to be from scratch. If using readymade pastry gives you the confidence to make a quiche then at least it is a step in the right direction to demystifying the process of cooking.

Certification overload

| Sarah Goler

| Department of Politics and International Studies, University of Warwick

Food certifications are common recipes composed of ingredients designed to relay helpful information to consumers about products.

Just braise one part food composition and one part scientific research, and then simmer until it has reached the desired food safety standard. Next, mix in a generous amount of government legislation, a dash of proper labeling, garnish with a certification mark and

voilà, the result is happy consumers contented by the assurances that they are purchasing high-quality, safe and nutritious foods. Certifications also provide a means of differentiating products, essential for competing in global marketplaces, and offer the individual a chance to support worthy causes such as sustainability, saving rainforests and feeding the hungry.

I spent a day wandering through numerous supermarkets in order to explore the various certifications present on labels today. There are a plethora of marks to appeal to everyone from meat abstainers - assured by Vegetarian Society Approved products, to nature lovers - Conservation Grade's Nature Friendly Farming, the Woodland Trust and Linking Environment and Farming (LEAF). Many products act as signboards displaying flags and nationalities that advertise German, Spanish and Italian Farm Assured meats, Controlled Origin (AOC) Swiss cheeses and Italian Denomination of Controlled Origin (DOC) olive oils.

Peruse the labels on adjacent items and you find the Marine Stewardship Council and Rainforest Alliance ensuring that your fish and other foods are sustainably farmed, as well as Fairtrade stamps affirming that developing country producers receive better deals in world trade. British Lion Quality and Assured Food Standards guarantee rigorous production principles, and there are packages displaying a variety of organic, bio and gluten free certifications from all over the world. In addition to these there are the bright red, blue and yellow European Protected Designation of Origin (PDO), Protected Geographical Indication (PGI) and Traditional Specialty Guaranteed (TSG) marks which certify the authenticity, quality and traditional nature of your cheeses, meats and other goods.

Amazingly, these are only a few among hundreds of different certifications circulating around the world; an article in the *Washington Post* states that there are currently around six-hundred 'eco-certifications'[1]. Certifications lead to positive impacts in many areas. However, difficulties arise as these formulas are extensively reproduced. The reliability and honesty of marks varies, and as they multiply they can be unrecognisable to consumers confronted with innumerable choices. Rather than being uncontestable methods to ensure consumer contentment, I believe too many certifications can overload the individual and become recipes for distress. Walking into a supermarket to acquire basic necessities is a normal part of everyday life in most parts of the western world, but is becoming radically more complicated. Nowadays one must take into account everything from nutrition, taste, type and cost to a wide variety of ethical, environmental and humanist issues. As the world becomes more interconnected the prevalence of

food certifications is likely to grow. What is important to keep in mind is that certifications are like political candidates, and it is important to critically analyse their claims and actions before electing to buy their products.

I have written the following recipe for 'certification style turkey and cottage cheese lasagna' in order to illustrate how complex over-certification can make a dish. Please do not feel obligated to use the exact brands I have listed. I have marked (in **bold**) generic ingredients that may be substituted with the product of your choice.

---

[1] Eilperin, J. Environmental certification becoming increasingly crowded and contested field. Washington Post [Internet]. 2010 May 03 [cited 2011 May 07]

Certification style turkey and cottage cheese lasagna:

Ingredients:

- 12 Decco certified durum wheat **lasagna** egg pasta **noodles** (more or less depending on noodle size)
- 15ml extra virgin **olive oil** PDO-certified Umbria Colli Martani
- 1 large Soil Association organic standard **yellow onion**, chopped
- 2 cloves Soil Association organic standard **garlic**, chopped
- 500g free range **minced turkey**
- 1 medium organic certified **courgette**, grated
- 750g Seeds of Change organic **tomato and basil sauce**
- 800g SO organic **chopped tomatoes**
- 142g SO organic **tomato puree**
- 644g natural **plain cottage cheese**
- 50g PDO-certified Parmigiano-Reggiano **(Parmesan) cheese**, grated
- 1 organic British free range **egg**, beaten
- 240g TSG-certified **Mozzarella** di Bufala, shredded by hand
- 120ml **water**
- 30ml Fairtrade natural golden granulated cane **sugar**
- 15ml Soil Association organic standard **oregano**
- 5ml Geo organic atlantic sea **salt**
- 2.5ml Bart Fairtrade black **pepper**

To make:

Heat oil in a large pot on medium. Add onion and sauté until clear, about 2 minutes. Add garlic and cook for another minute. Add turkey, break into small bits and cook through until browned. Mix in grated courgette. Gently stir in tomatoes with liquid, tomato paste and sauce. Add sugar, salt and pepper. Mix and bring to a boil, then simmer on low for one hour, stirring occasionally. Remove from heat.

Soak lasagna noodles in hot tap water for 20 minutes. Meanwhile, mix cottage cheese, parmesan, egg and oregano in a separate bowl.

To assemble, spread turkey mix (480ml) on a 22 × 33cm rectangular dish. Shake water off 6 noodles and lay across sauce. Spread half of cottage cheese mixture over noodles and top with 1/3 mozzarella. Spread more turkey filling (480ml) on top of cheese. Top with 6 more noodles, spread remaining cheese mixture and 1/3 mozzarella. Add last layer of meat sauce and sprinkle top with remaining mozzarella. Preheat oven to 180 C and bake covered with foil for 25 minutes. Remove foil and bake 25 minutes uncovered or until hot and bubbly. Stand 15 minutes before cutting.

City vines

| Richard Sharp
| Urban Wines

The Urban Wine Company was a crazy, hare-brained idea that started with the vision that it wanted to grow grapes and make wine in the middle of bustling London.

There were a few things that were required to make it happen and this included finding like-minded people who saw the advantages of city living and had an open-minded and lateral view on urban wine making. Critically, the Tooting wine makers saw that wine offered an opportunity for neighbours and friends to get together and to form a community of winemakers.

The first urban wine harvest was a modest affair with seven households involved in pooling their garden grapes. These were then taken down to a winery where they were trampled 'the old fashioned way', under foot and in a tin bath. An article covering the urban harvest

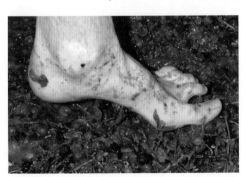

was featured in a national newspaper and a flood of interest followed that surprised the Urban Wine organisers. Deciding to move with the momentum, the Urban Wine Company was formed with the simple aim of producing a London wine. Over the last couple of years the Urban Wine Company has had over 200 members, all contributing their garden and allotment grapes. These are annually pressed and transformed into bottles of wine that are redistributed to their members. In 2010, 1,300 bottles were made from over a metric tonne of city-grown grapes.

From its early days as a small community project, thanks to the huge efforts of its largely voluntary staff, the Urban Wine Company has successfully created an infrastructure of community grape growers across the capital. The wine is now not only sold on to its members, but also offered for sale as a limited range in some specialist independent wine merchants in South West and South East London. The social infrastructure has also brought together a network of small and local drink and food producers including honey makers in Hackney and micro brewers in Mitcham.

My initial brain wave has been completely vindicated as sceptics originally thought the suggestion of producing a city wine was preposterous. During 2009, the urban blush was reviewed favourably by *Decanter magazine* and tasted live on BBC Radio 4's 'You &

Yours' programme. During the show I commented what we were doing was similar to the early days of punk rock, when you didn't need any great musical expertise to make music; you just had to have an enthusiasm and an open minded attitude.

At our annual wine tasting event, Urban Wine Company members swapped stories on their latest wine and how their vines have been faring during the recent hot weather conditions. From across North, South-East and West London, members lovingly cradled their bottles with personalised labels that celebrated the birth of new children or proudly represented the streets and neighbourhoods where the grapes were grown. This certainly represented a breed of urban wine makers who were fiercely proud of their London area, equal to the regional pride of rural food and drink producers in the UK and France.

The vision of the Urban Wine Company continues with a simple wish for more communities to live together and to be brought closer together through the mutual production of locally made wine. The ambitions for the Urban Wine movement grow steadily and new members are mailed their new vines by post. It's incredible to send out a few vines in a postal padded bag and then to visit our members in the future and see that these small packages have grown into fully fledged urban vineyards. It really is the power of the postal package. As well as populating the capital with new baby

vines, we're also planning on broadening the range of its wine and on making a London sparkling wine and a red in the near future.

The key ingredients for creating a movement that captures people's imagination are simple: believe in what you're doing, have a good partnership with community members, and have fun and be able to demonstrate that you have something that is worth getting people together for. In our case, it was wine produced from grapes that were going to waste that provided the galvanising force to cement community relationships and seal friendships.

If you're in Camden or Camberwell and you see a person walk past you wearing an Urban Wine t-shirt with the loud and proud logo 'Vino for Tooting', have a chat with them and ask them to point you in the direction of the nearest wine or vine. If they can't help you, look up at the clouds and it's just possible you might find a vine growing above your head. Our members will do anything to get their vines into the city.

Coronation chicken

I **Dr. Claire Dwyer**

I Department of Geography, UCL

For many people their experience of coronation chicken is a sweet, bright yellow filling to a bought sandwich. However, this dish of cold chicken and curry cream sauce has a rather interesting history which is illustrative of Britain's hybrid and post-colonial culinary cultures.

Coronation chicken was invented by Rosemary Hume for the banquet served to guests at the coronation of Queen Elizabeth II in 1953. Hume was the founder of the chic London Cordon Bleu Cookery School and the recipe was published in *The Constance Spry Cookery Book* in 1956. However, the origins of the dish probably go back to the Jubilee of George V in 1935 (when it was called, of course, 'Jubilee Chicken') and the combination of curry flavour, chicken and dried fruits such as apricots were said to be a favourite of Queen Adelaide (wife of William IV). It is this combination of dried fruits and spices from the empire which signals the colonial connections of this invented royal and national dish.

If one wants to understand the complex postcolonial legacies of empire in Britain one need look no further than the debates about our so-called national cuisine. It has become a truism to state that Britain's national dish is chicken *tikka masala*, which replaced fish and chips introduced into Britain by the Eastern European Jews of the East End. What is particularly interesting about the championing of chicken *tikka masala* is not simply the ways in which South Asian influences have been embraced by British diners, but the fusing of culinary cultures. Chicken *tikka masala* is not an Indian dish but is instead one invented through translation to satisfy British palates for the 'exotic'. It is the successor of other Anglo-Indian inventions such as mulligatawny soup and indeed coronation chicken. Both dishes make use of a specifically manufactured mix called 'curry powder' rather than the traditional blend of Indian spices (*garam masala*) now familiar to British cooks. These inventions remind us of the ways in which all national cuisines are 'invented traditions' and that it can be instructive to trace the trajectories and networks which shape what we celebrate as essentially British. Coronation chicken – invented to celebrate the crowning of the monarch - reflects the imperial trading networks which made spices and dried fruits a key part of the British diet from the seventeenth century onwards.

There are many different versions of this dish which is now being rediscovered in the enthusiasm for 'retro' cuisine. In the 1950s version of the recipe, the chicken, then a luxurious treat, was poached before being dressed in a spicy sauce of curried onions, red wine, tomato puree, lemon, apricot purée, mayonnaise and double cream. Contemporary versions use lighter sauces and often serve the chicken on a bed of rice or crunchy lettuce.

My own version (last made as a contribution to a street party to celebrate the 2011 Royal Wedding) is a combination of various tastes and preferences. I often add chopped celery, spring onions or chopped grapes.

Coronation chicken:

Ingredients:
Cooked cold chicken (poached in spices like cinnamon, pepper, ginger and saffron)
50g chopped apricots
2 tbsp curry powder (dry roasted)
2 tsp Worcestershire sauce
5 tbsp mango chutney
200ml mayonnaise
200ml Greek yoghurt
50g flaked almonds
Coriander (chopped)

To make:
Mix all the ingredients except the almonds and coriander to make a sauce and then combine this with the chicken (cut into pieces). Refrigerate for a couple of hours.

Stir through the coriander and then sprinkle with the almonds. Serve with green salad and basmati rice.

Creating compassion

I **Marleen Slingenbergh**
I UCL Vegetarian Society

Vegetarians and vegans have a bit of a loony reputation. In universities, it may not help when groups of students form official 'vegetarian societies' to organise activities together.

My involvement in such a society has frequently attracted friendly fun-poking of which my favourite is when our society is dubbed the 'UCL hippy support group'. But I am convinced that any attention given to the idea of vegetarianism is good attention, because it encourages people to challenge their dietary choices. The strains of industrial farming have become so large that no individual can justify not considering at least cutting down, if not altogether abandoning, their consumption of animal products.

Let me introduce you to the elephant in the room, as he is thumping around to get your attention. His name is the Meat Crisis. I understand that with cries about man-made climate change, pandemic threats, unmanageable population increase, uncontrollable food prices and general impending doom echoing across the globe, you may be experiencing slight 'crisis fatigue' and it is hard to see which issues merit your attention most. The good news is that they are all intricately related to our elephant here,

and controlling the amount of meat, dairy and eggs one consumes has a large and direct impact.

As an example, consider the close but under-appreciated relationship between infectious diseases and animal domestication. Since the beginning of human evolution, the first major period of disease probably started in the Eastern Mediterranean roughly twelve millennia ago, where domestication began. Human measles, for example, most likely emerged from a rinderpest-type virus of sheep and goats, while human influenza may have only arisen about 4500 years ago with the domestication of waterfowl. Over the last few decades, there has been a dramatic resurgence of infectious diseases. Major international bodies including the World Health Organisation predict that as demands for animal protein are increasing around the globe, animal agriculture will keep intensifying and the emergence of infectious diseases will keep increasing.

Intensive agriculture aids the spread of disease in several ways. There is the obvious effect of closer proximity between animals which gives more opportunities for pathogens to move between animals. There is also the underestimated effect of extreme confinements on the immune systems of animals, which are suppressed by increased stress levels. The modern strain of the swine flu virus was first discovered in a farm in Sampson County, North Carolina, the county with the highest pig population in the United States, confining more than 2 million pigs. The farm was a breeding facility that confined thousands of sows in sow stalls, metal cages that are so small that pigs cannot turn around in them. Crated sows have been reported to have higher stress levels and

impaired immune systems[1]. Measures as simple as providing animals with the mercy of straw bedding so that they are saved from the immune-suppressive stress of lying on bare concrete their whole lives have been shown to lower disease transmission rates.

There are several other aspects of the meat crisis that call for urgent attention. In summary they are: the rapidly increasing emissions of greenhouse gases emerging from the entire meat cycle; the water footprint of animal products; the effect of animal production on biodiversity; the problems of animal welfare; and the implications of meat production for human health.

Most people alive eat ten times as much meat as their great-grandparents did. It is not so much the act of eating meat that is having dramatic consequences, but rather the sheer number of animals we are rearing and consuming. The ethics of meat consumption have long surpassed the question of whether it is right to kill an animal. That said, in a world where we are surrounded by shops and restaurants that offer an abundance of affordable animal products, abstinence is not easy. But every meat-free meal helps. On that note, I leave you a simple but delicious animal-product-free recipe, well tried and tested.

Vegan cupcakes:

Ingredients:

1 tbsp vinegar
1 ½ cups soymilk
2 ¾ cups self raising flour
2 tsp baking powder
½ tsp baking soda
1 cup sugar or syrup
½ cup oil (nut oils are nice but any will do)
1 tsp vanilla extract

To make:

Preheat the oven to 180 degrees Celsius. Put the vinegar into a small bowl and add the soymilk. Stir well and put to one side to let it curdle. Stir together the flour, sugar, baking powder, baking soda. If you want chocolate cupcakes, add cacao at this stage. Stir the oil and vanilla extract into the bowl containing the soymilk and vinegar. Add the wet ingredients to the dry ingredients and beat together. Spread the batter into paper cupcake holders with about ¼ cup of batter. Bake for 20-25 minutes. If you fancy it add icing of your choice!

[1] Greger, M., 2010., 'Industrial Animal Agriculture's Role in the Emergence and Spread of Disease' in J. D'Silva and J. Webster (Eds.) *The Meat Crisis*. Earthscan: London, p.166

Digger barley

| Hannah Roberson

| MA Anthropology of Food, SOAS

Mentoring new gardeners growing their own fruit and vegetables has presented some interesting challenges, but I wasn't prepared for barley. It's not one of your standard allotment crops.

I asked around, but none of the gardeners I knew had any experience of growing cereals. My new friend had trusted me to guide her through the tricky process of turning these seeds into barley and back into seeds again.

These weren't just ordinary seeds, either. She had been given some 'Digger Barley' seeds which were descended from barley grown on land occupied by the Diggers in the 17th century. The Diggers saw the devastating effects of enclosure, where common land was fenced in and the titles were formally held by private property owners. This ended a lot of traditional agricultural practices such as common grazing rights and arable farming in open fields, and disrupted the social fabric of the English countryside which in turn fuelled the industrial revolution by creating a large surplus rural population who could migrate to towns to work in factories. The Diggers planted food crops on common land in various parts of the country as an act of resistance to the early processes of industrialisation and privatisation.

Their vision of egalitarian rural communities and communal land ownership was crushed by landowners and the government, but the movement remains a powerful symbol for food movements. Their name was borrowed by the San Francisco Diggers, part of the 1960s counterculture movement which rejected mainstream values, including agricultural intensification and the proliferation of large supermarkets and heavily processed food in the post-war period. The San Francisco Diggers had a vision of a Free City and distributed free food, including the wholemeal Digger Bread baked in coffee cans. *Diggers and Dreamers* is a guide to communal living in the UK. Many communes have an ecological or self-sufficiency focus.

The symbolic power of the Diggers is strengthened by holding in our hands the seeds that they cultivated. Thinking of the dedicated farmers or gardeners who planted and tended the crops and saved the seeds over hundreds of years, it seemed right to share the seeds with other food-growers. The seeds also contained a timely message about the importance of public space, community agriculture and maintaining genetic diversity through saving seeds.

The modern industrial agri-food system is the logical descendent of enclosure. Private companies and shareholders profit from the corporate-driven system, and individual consumers may benefit from low prices and (the illusion of) convenience, but the public cost – financial and non-financial – is huge. Tax-payers foot the bill for cleaning up the environmental damage from industrial agriculture. Government subsidies support farmers' incomes and disguise the scandalously low prices that supermarkets pay to producers. Already stretched public health services need to find a way to cope with the consequences of diet-related ill-health.

Alternative food movements want to produce tasty and healthy food that is ecologically sustainable and does not exploit farmers. Because of the way the food system is structured, this cannot currently compete on price with food from industrial systems which benefit from economies of scale or processed food which enables companies to charge large mark-ups. This means the products of alternative systems are mostly accessible to wealthy elites or those with the time and inclination to seek out suppliers, buy in bulk or produce their own. To spread the benefits of good quality food more widely, food movements have emphasised the social benefits of community-based agriculture. Gardens have sprung up in schools, libraries, parks, doctors' surgeries and railway stations, public spaces which do not exist to make a profit but to provide vital services and promote wellbeing in a community.

Some public and charity funding is available to support these projects, but this is drying up. If public services are privatised or closed, or if there are any changes in ownership or institutional structure which might require these spaces to turn a profit, these community gardens would be threatened. Good quality food would be out of many people's reach. It is easy to see why the Diggers' planting barley on common land was a radical political act, and the goals of modern food movements may not be that far from theirs. The few seeds we planted may not produce much grain, but they connect us to a historical and global movement working to build democracy and social justice into the food system, starting with the simple act of planting seeds on public land.

Does it have to be this way?

l **Ruchi Tripathi**

l Action Aid International

Recipe for transition to sustainable agriculture – *'Hmmm...What is that'*, I hear you ask.

The idea of transition is that it is a journey without an end. Every system can be made more sustainable, as long as you embark on that journey and recognise that every small step you take along the way can make a difference.

Food connects the earth with its inhabitants. Human beings were able to prosper and multiply when they followed settled agriculture instead of hunting and gathering for their food. This shift 10,000 years ago was significant as it allowed humans to domesticate wild plants and animals, and increase their level of food production. Today, the earth's carrying capacity is being tested due to increasing environmental pressures made worse by unsustainable human activity.

This historic conquering of Mother Earth and nature was accelerated in early 1960s and 70s through the Green Revolution, which was promoted zealously by governments and research institutes, at times in collaboration with private corporations. Although it did manage to raise yields - provided the necessary inputs were available to increase food production – it came at the expense of long term sustainability of the soils, water, seeds, ecosystems, and human and animal health, not to mention the impact on cultural and spiritual aspects of food.

Peasants' organisations and millions of smallholder women and men farmers have been practicing sustainable agriculture for millennia, and an equally large number of them have entered the chemical treadmill due to either: a) the subsidies available on chemical fertilisers; or b) the availability of improved seeds that have further narrowed the genetic diversity of cultivated species.

There is a realisation amongst peasants and their movements that they have to fight for and protect their way of agro-ecological production. There is also recognition amongst some farmers on this chemical treadmill that there is a more sustainable system. Currently, incentives by the public and private sector such as subsidised seed and fertiliser

packages, proprietary seeds sold along with chemicals, and advertising by seed and chemical companies, are encouraging farmers to choose uniform seeds that will further narrow their genetic base, and to use chemicals and fertilisers that may address a problem in the short term without further thoughts about the long term consequences.

Those who are farming sustainably in developing countries are being lured to give up this way of farming as the market, governments, and media do not reward it. In order to overhaul this incentive system, we need a recipe that can have wide appeal. For systemic change, we need several entry points. For example, the current UK drought is an opportunity for UK farmers and food producers to think of working in synchronicity with nature, and to think more deeply about the health of their soil, water and resource conservation, and seed preservation.

For countries with large farming populations, the choice is clear. Producers need to be supported to farm sustainably using their knowledge and expertise. They could choose to farm sustainably if there were enough incentives to reform agricultural extension agencies, support research systems, create subsidies and address concerns about the unjust control of the food and farming system by corporations. Agriculture-led development is among the most sustainable methods of reducing poverty, particularly when women are at the forefront.

Even for countries like the UK – where less than 1.5% of the population is employed in agriculture and agriculture's share of the GDP is less than 1% – the core ingredients of the recipe remain the same: need for good soil health; diverse and nutritious foods based on diverse seeds; water conservation and sustainable use. To popularise this recipe, we need to tap into our concerns for eating healthily, our innate concern for the environment, our physical isolation as an island and our love of gardening and allotments. It is intriguing for me that in spite of celebrity gardeners and amazing flower shows, we don't celebrate farming and food providers in this country. We each need to take this on board and engage in a debate on how our food is produced, how the current food system provides very little incentive to grow sustainably, and how as consumers we can make choices that help provide a sustainable income for farmers.

Remember to check on the label of the food you are eating for indicators of the product's sustainability: its impact on the ecology (soil, water, biodiversity); on the community and livelihoods of food producers (their control over their produce, their share of the value of that produce); on the health of the consumers (pesticide residue, nutritional content post processing); and the impact of fossil fuel-based production and distribution in an oil-constrained world.

Eating cats

I Mark Carnall

I Grant Museum of Zoology, UCL

Eating our furry companions, including cats and dogs, may seem at first barbaric and, oxymoronically, inhumane. However, it is only from a privileged viewpoint that eating moggies may seem in any way unsavoury.

In fact, as I hope to demonstrate, cats and other four legged friends are perhaps among the few sustainable meats left on the planet.

Irreversible damage to natural environments and exploitation of finite resources in the pursuit of food continues apace and is only set to increase as the world human population swells past seven billion, predicted to top ten billion in the next forty years. The world's fauna and flora are directly spoiled through the hunting and taking of wild plants and animals. In many parts of the world exotic animals and plants are critically endangered not because they form a part of traditional diets but because people living in starvation are turning to all manner of different food stuffs (according to the FAO an estimated 14% of the world is undernourished). Environments are indirectly spoiled as they are turned over from bio-diverse ecosystems to land suitable for agriculture and livestock.

You don't have to travel the world to see how much natural wildlife is being destroyed. Much of the picturesque English countryside is in fact farmland – about as natural as inner city parks. The world's oceans are the most severely affected in humans' unending hunger. Numerous species are overfished despite scientific evidence that predicts either population collapses or, worse, a complete ecosystem crash turning the once rich oceans into nothing more than an aquatic desert. Of particular concern isn't just the fact that the world population continues to grow. Especially in developing countries like India and China, the key problem is if these countries start to develop diets and tastes as broad and big as the western world.

So how could adding cats to our menus help the natural world? Chiefly – second only to our particular species - cats, dogs and various other pet species cause widespread environmental damage and destruction. Humans insist on taking pets with them as they spread across the globe. Introduced animals hunt and kill native species, particularly birds and small mammals or outcompete native species for resources. Escaped animals can establish feral populations which damage ecosystems even without a human presence. Pets will bring with them their own diseases and parasites which can devastate wild animal populations which cannot adapt to the spreading of alien pathogens that have evolved in another part of the world. Furthermore, as if our own food industry wasn't damaging enough, there is a pet food industry which also causes damage to the natural world through exploitation and pollution. How can we feel justified in a world where some people's pets have a better quality of life than 14% of our fellow humans?

If we surmounted illogical and cultural food taboos and added cat to our diets we could reduce the damage done by an overpopulation of cats to the natural environment. In parts of the world like Australia, feral cats are rampant and are impossible to control without sustained hunting. Perhaps the most pathetic aspects of our food culture are foodstuffs which are considered delicacies. Wild caviar and shark fin soup are two well documented examples. Harvesting for these dishes is unethical, unsustainable, illegal and worst of all, the ingredients do not actually add much to the dishes they are used in. With a

slight re-tweaking of our tastes we could push these dishes off of our restaurant menus. Cat tail soup is a far more sustainable and ethical alternative to shark fin soup and battered kitty and chips on a Friday night would give the world's cod stocks a last gasp chance of recovery.

Education with pesto

I **Sarah Moore**

I Sarah Moore Caterers

This recipe is the one I pull out when I'm doing a demonstration in front of tough audiences. When I say tough audiences I am referring to a group that let you know they are hard to please and what ever you make had better be interesting and why are you here showing us how to cook anyway?

I've done my share of these gigs where I'm roasting in front of a community gathering, where a good sort from the Local Authority has thrown me to the lions to deliver a healthy cooking demonstration in the middle of an estate.

The remarkable moral of this story is proof of the power of food; culinary diplomacy. When I make food from nettles, everyone stops in their tracks to see this scary, bad weed that everyone knows, recognizes and avoids at all costs. The nettle pesto demonstration takes less than 3 minutes start to finish. Once they have tried this little nettle canapé served on some French bread, they are enthralled and want to know more about it, and engage in recapping on the method, 'how long do you boil it?' 'how much do you use?' 'actually my mum used to eat that when she was a girl, we didn't believe her'. The stories and anecdotes flow.

How strange it is that in this un-shockable world we live in, it is nature that stops people in their tracks and makes them take a step backwards at the idea of nettles being so delicious and versatile. People become delighted by this trick.

Nettle pesto:

Ingredients:

125g freshly picked nettles (tops only and not in seed)
2 cloves of garlic
As much chili as you wish (I used 3 bird's eye chili)
50g of any nuts (brazils, cashews, walnuts, hazelnuts, pine)
75g of hard cheese (like Parmesan)
120ml virgin rapeseed oil (or olive)
Flaky sea salt and ground pepper (Essex sea salt)

To make:

1. Blanch the nettles in boiling water for 1 minute, chill in cold water and drain.
2. In a blender place the garlic, nuts, oil and blitz to a smooth paste then add the nettles.
3. Add the grated cheese and blitz again.
4. Season to your taste.
5. Put in a clean jar and it will keep in the fridge for about 3 weeks.

Mix into hot pasta, or new potatoes lightly crushed. Delicious served on bread as a snack.

When I'm out picking nettles people always stop and engage, ask me what I am doing and why. When you are collecting food from the wild, even if it is in an urban park or harvesting from a stray bramble, you are rendered 'safe' in this activity and people are more likely to interact.

Nettles are a nutritious food source, high in vitamins (including A and D) and minerals (including calcium, iron, magnesium and potassium). Just two generations ago, it was commonplace to eat boiled nettles as the greens served with a meal.

Consider the following possibilities:

Nettle risotto
Nettle tortilla
Potato and nettle cakes shallow fried
Nettle soup
Nettle tea

When collecting nettles, do so wearing gloves and just collect the tops (4-6cm). Do not collect near roadsides or where dogs may have urinated. The ideal nettle season is late January through to April, May, although I use them every year until July. When their tops have gone to seed, do not use them. There is another opportunity in October when there is a second crop.

Eight Treasure pudding

I **Dr. Vivienne Lo**
I Department of History, UCL

I first ate Eight Treasure pudding in a Washington restaurant with Auntie B-C and one of the Wei family aunties. Auntie B-C had had to order in advance because to achieve the right consistency you have to steam the pudding for over an hour.

And it wasn't New Year, the usual time to serve this immortal of all comfort foods. Nevertheless it was a kind of celebration – a reunion, although we hadn't actually met before.

From the mid-nineteenth century the Wei and the Lo families had been intricately connected. Both great-grandfathers had played important roles in building the first modern Chinese dockyards on the banks of the Min River in Fuzhou city. The next generation of Wei girls and Lo boys all grew up in great luxury playing together in the tea

Eight Treasure pudding:
Prepare well in advance as the un-steamed pudding will mature with age for up to four days in the refrigerator.

Ingredients:
550g glutinous rice
4 tablespoons of oil
lard or butter for greasing the bowl
3 tsp sugar
420g sweet red bean paste
25g walnuts and/or *ginko* nuts
6 tsp candied and dried fruit; in particular angelica, cherries, lychee, *longan* and *jujube*

To make:
Wash the rice and place in a saucepan. Cover with 1 cm water. Bring to boil and simmer gently for 30 minutes adding more water if it seems to be sticking. Add the oil and all the sugar, turn and stir until well mixed. Meanwhile soften the red bean paste by placing in a pan of hot water for 30 minutes. Grease the sides of a large heatproof basin or bowl heavily with fat. Stick the nuts and candied or dried fruits in a pattern on the sides and bottom of the basin. Divide the rice into four portions and the bean paste into three portions. Place a layer of sweetened rice in the basin, then spread a thinner layer of sweet bean paste on top of the rice.

Repeat the layers, finishing with a rice layer and packing the mixture down into the bowl. Cover the basin and refrigerate.

When the pudding is needed place the whole basin into a covered steamer and steam steadily for at least one and a half hours in the manner in which you would cook Christmas pudding. Invert the basin on to a large round heated serving dish to turn out the pudding. Decorate with extra fruit.

traders' villas where they lived in the hills south of the river. Eventually many of them intermarried, breeding a team of double cousins.

After the 1949 revolution the family were flung to all corners of the world, some to become captains of industry and commerce, others to a life on the streets, and others to die violently. My sister and I rarely met our Chinese relatives when we were growing up; only our branch of the Lo family had ended up in London. When we did meet up with the cousins and their offspring it often became an opportunity for the old folk to relive their enchanted childhood.

Eight Treasure pudding is gooey and substantial; glutinous rice is good for sticking families together. Unlike the heavy and sickly sweet European suet puddings, like spotted dick and treacle pudding, it is served alongside savoury dishes: sweet and savoury are not thought of as contradictory when served together in one course. I usually make a great big pudding for everyone to tuck in to, but that day in Washington we each had our own small individual bowls.

There are many dimensions to this pudding. The Eight Treasures refer to the rice, red beans and dried fruit and nut ingredients you choose to use in your pudding. These commonly include: lotus seeds, *jujube*, preserved kumquat, *longan* fruit, candied cherries, candied winter melon, Job's tears, and melon seeds, finished off with slivers of red and green plum. The Eight Treasures are also the eight objects that the Eight Daoist Immortals hold in their hands. These are variously defined as precious pearls, auspicious sceptres and coins, and magical whisks. They have a Buddhist incarnation as the different ribbons and knots of lucky charms associated with good fortune, marital harmony, healthy offspring, happiness, longevity, and all the things that have traditionally made a Chinese life worth living.

Over and above the intrigue with these divinities and the registers of good fortune, like all Chinese foods the flavours of each of the Eight Treasures are traditionally thought to carry nutritional potency. Red bean paste, for example, is a sweet/sour tonic credited with diuretic properties, while sticky rice is a blood and *Qi* tonic with the colour of jade, which signifies prosperity. Many of the dried fruits are ascribed therapeutic qualities. Walnut is thought to be good for the kidneys and brain (the sections of the nut look like the kidneys or two halves of the brain). *Ginko* seeds are traditionally categorised as bitter sweet, they nourish the lungs and are now used worldwide as a memory tonic. Being well steamed, Eight Treasure pudding is also easy to digest, so you can serve it to the old and sick as a restorative food. Only last month at a house-warming banquet for my martial arts teacher in the mountains of Sichuan, at the epicentre of the 2008 earthquake (his house and school had collapsed), I sat next to his master, a 103 year old Daoist with a hearty appetite. As I watched him wolf down plate loads of sweet glutinous rice, between cigarettes, he told me how he still trains three hours a day and can thread a needle without glasses.

These days at New Year festival it is Neil Murphy, my son-in-law, a nutritionist and father of my forthcoming grandchild, who has taken over the pudding making. Perhaps, after all, it will be Neil's job to bind together the next generation of our family!

Financialised food

I Christine Haigh

I World Development Movement

Back in the 19th century, 'futures markets' for crops such as maize and wheat were set up to allow US farmers and buyers of food, such as millers and bakers, to protect themselves from changing prices.

In the 1930s, following the Wall Street Crash, regulations were put in place to limit the involvement in these markets of banks and other financial institutions that had no interest in the food that was being sold, but were simply out to make profits.

These regulations stayed in place until the 1990s, when they were severely weakened by lobbying from banks such as Goldman Sachs and Barclays Capital (the investment arm of the high street bank).

Subsequently, recent years have seen the number of contracts traded on these markets increase fivefold, and food prices have become increasingly volatile, hitting record highs, as in the food price crisis of 2007-8. Though other factors such as climate change and demand for biofuels are also contributing to higher food prices, speculation rides on the back of changes in supply and demand, exacerbating food price spikes.

For example, in summer 2010, following a drought in Russia that caused wildfires and damaged the wheat crop, the price of wheat skyrocketed. Yet with a bumper crop in the US, the global wheat harvest was the third highest on record: there was no shortage of wheat. The price spike was due to speculators piling into the market, anticipating a shortage and looking to make a quick buck.

Similarly, between April 2010 and April 2011, the value of futures contracts for maize owned by financial institutions such as hedge funds and investment banks increased by 127.5% to $15.7 billion. In the same period, the price of maize itself – Africa's most important staple food – increased by 102%.

While this type of profiteering is affecting people's grocery bills around the world, the greatest impact of food speculation is felt by the poorest people in developing countries, who typically spend between 50 and 90% of their

income on food. As a result of rising prices, many families have to cut back on food, use up savings, or cut back on other essentials such as health care and education.

The good news is that in 2010, the US passed new regulations to prevent excessive speculation on food, and the European Union is bringing forward similar proposals. Food speculation has even made it on to the agenda of the G20 leaders.

The World Development Movement has been calling on the UK Government to support proposals from the European Union to regulate the commodity markets to prevent excessive speculation. The bad news is that with the UK's historic tendency to favour "light touch" regulation, it's been challenging. We need everyone who wants to see a food system that serves people rather than profits to join the fight.

Focusing on screwpines

I **Shuen-Yi Long**
I UCL Medical School

As a melting pot of Southeast Asia, the Malaysian food scene has undergone plenty of evolution over the centuries. The diverse society of the country is the legacy of British colonialism and trade relations with neighbouring nations.

One notable example of cultural fusion is the Peranakan Chinese culture, which developed from traditional Chinese and Malay cultures around the 15th-16th centuries, a long time before my own family settled in British colonial Malaya. I could write pages about how Malaysia's history of trade, colonialism, immigration and the resultant meeting of different cultures have produced a delicious cultural legacy that has a unique identity of its own, but my focus here is mainly on the Malaysian obsession with food and how culturally determined tastes can have an impact on social life and health.

Malaysians tend to favour bold flavours in their food; chilli, onion, garlic, *belachan* (a pungent shrimp paste), coconut and tamarind are just a few of the favoured ingredients. Food unites Malaysians through shared tastes and local ingredients. The social life of a Malaysian revolves around sharing meals

Bubur pulut hitam:
(Peranakan Chinese black glutinous rice pudding)

Ingredients:
200g of black glutinous rice*
1 screwpine (*pandan*) leaf*

*Black glutinous rice and *pandan* leaves can be found at most Chinese supermarkets.

To make:
Rinse the rice and place in a large pot with 1 litre of water and a knotted screwpine leaf. Cook over low heat for 1-2 hours, stirring occasionally until the rice is soft and you get a thick rice pudding. Add sugar to taste, cover the pot and let simmer for another 20 minutes. Serve warm in bowls with a drizzle of coconut milk.

with family and friends. Even watching football matches with friends at a local eatery over a supper of *roti canai* (a griddled flatbread better known as *paratha*), *dhal* curry and *teh tarik* (milk tea that is 'pulled' from one cup to another before serving) becomes a ritual of bonding. So what dish represents the tastes of Malaysians in the global food forum? Although many Malaysians consider the national dish to be *nasi lemak*: coconut rice served with spicy *sambal* (chilli paste), peanuts, fried anchovies, cucumber slices and a boiled egg, another dish that I think deserves equal attention is *bubur pulut hitam*. This Southeast Asian version of rice pudding is a Peranakan Chinese specialty made with black glutinous rice boiled with sugar and *pandan* (screwpine) leaves; then served with generous amounts of coconut milk. I remember this dessert from childhood and it is a staple treat from many Malaysian Chinese and Malay kitchens. Being both high in sugar and fat, *bubur pulut hitam* is a testimony to the sweet tooth shared by many Malaysians all over the world and also a nod to the diet-related problems that Malaysia faces in an age of sedentary lifestyles, an abundance of food and the increasing popularity of palm oil in national cuisine, mainly through deep-frying and processed foods.

The urban Malaysian love affair with food and its central role in everyday social life has a dark side to it as well: the increasing rates of obesity, diabetes and heart disease being proof of what our habit of late night suppers, high fat intake and the national sweet tooth has led to. It is difficult for Malaysians to let go of favourite dishes such as *nasi lemak*, *roti canai* or *bubur pulut hitam* as food and eating are so central to Malaysian identity and social life. However, there is a movement towards healthier eating among urban Malaysians, particularly after diet-related health issues became a popular topic of discussion in the media, the medical community, local communities and even the Ministry of Health with campaigns encouraging Malaysians to reduce their intake of fat, salt and sugar. What I would take from all this as a medical student is that making the urban Malaysian diet as healthy as possible can be done but has to be handled with care and an understanding of the situation at hand. The clever use of local produce and ingredients in the kitchen to produce healthier versions of national favourites and the knowledge that moderation when it comes to the occasional bowl of *bubur pulut hitam* means that the Malaysian love of food need not clash with health agendas.

Food directions

| **Dræyk van der Hørn**
| Bonnington Café

Food is central to so many of the greatest moments in our lives. From festivals marking important events and the seasons of the year, to the everyday food that sustains our basic activity and health, our relationship with food is one of the most important relationships we have.

A revolution in our relationship with food is the basis for a revolution in our relationships with each other and our connection with the planet. We have a chance to decide on a future that makes food central to how we as individuals and citizens of this planet can take positive action for change.

It's simple, we all eat and every plate of food has a story, and it's a story we all share.

We all love a bit of salt and pepper on our food. Nothing much in that is there? It helps flavour the food, that's all, or is it?

Consider this: pepper is a spice that has been cultivated for millennia. It was considered more precious than gold and traded as such in medieval Europe. Trade routes were forged, wars fought,

ships sunk all because of this simple "seed". What a history!

But this is also the story of our times. From the cost of fuel (and pollution created) to ship it to the UK (in fact peppercorns are the most widely traded spice in the world) to the poor wages given to workers and farmers, the spice trade is increasingly controlled by large multi-national companies who put profit before anything else.

It's also a story about flavour. Pepper is a true revelation to the taste buds and a healing spice in many medicines. There are over 100 varieties of peppercorn, but why is it all we find available in the shops is black, white and pink? Peppercorns offer a myriad of flavours and only a small amount can change your life forever.

This little tale is about thinking about where our food comes from and how it impacts on our lives. Food connects us to the past, the present and the future. We have choices! And we have a voice!

But the revolution in food is also about much, much more. It's about asking ourselves some important questions and rising to the challenges of finding answers. Can we develop places where we can work together? Can we imagine a space where simple ideas come together? Can we create "hubs" where food is celebrated?

My passion comes from a lifetime of teaching myself to grow my own food, to cook and build community based on the central principle that we all eat. So let's do it well and share! Through communication, connection, and community building, food can be brought to our tables from sustainable sources and through fair trade that realises the value of everyone on the food chain and preserves and honours the planet.

Every "hub" will be shaped by the community that fosters it, and by the needs and desires of the people who live nearby, and reaching out and responding, hand in hand, to local and global needs. Each hub would be part of a greater web of inspiration that nurtures all by celebrating creativity and innovation.

The next Green Revolution to feed the planet must be a local and human scale one, led by all as citizens of the planet (that's you!), not just as consumers, suppliers or by standing on the sidelines while others decide what they think is good for us!

Take control, eat and change your life!

Harira soup:

This is a spicy and lovely autumnal dish – it is traditionally served after Ramadan to break the long fast as it's full of protein (usually meat!) – but here is your plant-based variation... still rich and a good booster to boot!

Ingredients:

3 onions
3 cloves of garlic
1 cup of chickpeas
1 cup of red lentils
10 tomatoes
1 red pepper
2 tbsp tomato puree
1 carrot or squash (or seasonal vegetable)
1 lemon
1 tbsp cumin seeds
1 tsp ginger root
1 tsp turmeric, paprika, ground sumac, thyme, and oregano
A few bay leaves

To make:

Fry the chopped onions with the garlic in a little oil. Add the cumin seeds and ginger root (finely chopped); fry until the aroma is released then add 1 heaped tsp each of turmeric, paprika, ground sumac, thyme, oregano and then about one litre of stock water. Allow this to simmer for about five minutes.

Add the cooked chickpeas, lentils, chopped tomatoes, tomato puree, diced red bell pepper and a dash of cayenne pepper. Let this cook for 25 minutes.

Add diced carrot, squash or any seasonal vegetables you like. Add salt and pepper to taste and lots of bay leaves and juice of a lemon.

Cook and cook this... for at least an hour! It only gets better the longer it simmers! Do it the day before and re-heat for best results.

Serve this with lots of fresh chopped tomatoes and herbs.

Bake pita breads and cover with *Zatar* (spicy sesame, thyme and sumac berry) or garlic oil!

A really warming yet perfect summer soup!

Food sovereignty

I **Michelle Springfield**
I Royal Holloway, University of London

Perhaps the most disturbing feature of modern global society is the glaring disparity between those who have too much to eat and those who do not have enough.

In 2010, 925 million people around the world were undernourished, that is to say that they were lacking in some, or all, nutritional elements necessary for human health[1]. At the same time it is estimated that 1 in 6 of the world's population eat too much[2].

The fact is that the world produces enough food to feed everyone, but the main problem is that many people in the world do not have either access or ownership of land on which to grow it, or sufficient income to buy it. Nor do they often have a say on what is grown and for whom. When we consume products such as coffee, fresh fruit or vegetables we are often participating in a global process; it may feel like an individual experience but it is increasingly a social,

[1] Figures from the UN FAO (2010)

[2] Around a billion people are overweight of which more than 300 million are clinically obese. Figures from WHO (2011)

political and environmental act with unintended consequences.

This is not a modern dilemma. It is fair to say that throughout history food has been one of the principal sources of power and its importance felt at all levels of society, from those who suffer directly from want of sustenance to those whose authority, security or profits depend on its supply. Food can therefore be considered as power in its most basic and tangible form.

The reasons why so many go hungry in a world of plenty are complex but one factor is always relevant. That factor is power. The 'right to food' was recognised as a universal human right more than 50 years ago but this has not eradicated the problem of food insecurity in any long-term sense. Indeed, if the current global food system remains the same, the problem of food inequality is likely to become worse in the future. So what can be done to improve the situation?

This is where the idea of 'food sovereignty' could be a recipe for change. Food sovereignty is an extension of the right to food in that it demands democratic autonomy for people with respect to food in a way that the right to food does not. Aid agencies could guarantee the right to food without any input or control by those whose food needs are not being met. This can, and indeed has, resulted in total dependency on food aid for some food-vulnerable communities. Food sovereignty, by contrast, involves

the right to consume and produce food and a range of other sub-rights, including land rights, so it is a more complex and ambitious idea than the simple right to food.

Unlike the top down approach, associated with the failed attempts of international institutions such as the International Monetary Foundation and the World Trade Organization, the concept of food sovereignty proposes that every country and people should have the right to establish their own policies with regard to their food and agriculture system, providing these policies do not harm developing countries.

This requires a rebuilding and strengthening of local food systems, and putting people and the environment, instead of corporate profits, at the centre of rural development. Food sovereignty offers a way, through the democratic process, to empower those whose lives are blighted by hunger and transform them into active agents of change.

All over the world hundreds of thousands of producers and consumers are actively organizing for their right to healthy and culturally appropriate food produced through ecologically sound and sustainable methods. Social movements for land reform, indigenous rights, ethical trade, farmers' markets, community-supported agriculture, inner-city gardens and neighbourhood-food systems development, are a few examples of the widespread, multi-faceted efforts for food sovereignty. These organisations are all working towards transforming the social will of rural and urban movements into political will.

| Graciela Romero Vasquez
| War on Want

Food sovereignty strongly opposes corporate-driven agriculture and the transnational companies that are destroying people and nature.

It defends small-scale sustainable agriculture as a way to promote social justice and dignity. In Latin America, *Soberania Alimentaria* states that the control over our food systems should be in the hands of local people; it demands the right of people to define their own agricultural and food policies.

Food sovereignty asks us to think about six main elements that, when combined, make the right recipe to feed the world in a more sustainable, just and democratic manner.

These six elements are:
- To focus on food for all people
- To value and support food providers
- The localisation of food systems (bringing consumers and producers together)
- Placing local control over territory, land, grazing, water, seeds and fish populations
- Building small producers' knowledge and skills
- Working with nature using diverse, agro-ecological production and harvesting methods

Food Sovereignty does not call for people to be isolated in their communities or countries. However, it rejects governance structures, agreements and practices that depend on and promote unsustainable and inequitable international trade and give power to unaccountable corporations.

There is a growing consensus that control of our food system needs to be devolved to small-scale producers, local markets and women, who are already significantly contributing to feeding the world with the limited resources they have. If the world's population is going to eat in 2050 we will need the current 1.5 billion peasants, plus 800 million people growing food in urban gardens, 410 million gathering the hidden harvest of our forests and savannas, 190 million pastoralists and well over 100 million peasant fishers.

Food production should be centred at the heart of communities and families, not at the heart of profit-ridden corporations. There are millions of peasants in Africa, Asia and Latin America who are demonstrating that the way out of this crisis is through sustainable agro-ecological methods which can give us enough food to feed people while protecting the environment.

The Women Farmers' Society in Sri Lanka, working with the Movement for National Land and Agrarian Reform, tells us their own story of how food sovereignty is practiced. By using only agro-ecological methods and building the skills and knowledge of women, they have been able to produce food to feed their families as well as to sell in local markets. One of its members, Madu-rani, explains:

"It's not only about producing food but also the way it is produced and the impact that it has on our com-munity. There are more than 200 small farmers working with eco-sys-tems now. In addition, we [women] are also more valued and involved in decisions affecting our community".

War on Want is committed to building the global movement for food sovereign-ty. Together with our partner organi-sations and other allies within La Via Campesina, we call on all people to join the millions of small farmers, fisher-folks, pastoralists, indigenous peoples and consumers across the globe who are demanding adoption of the food sovereignty framework. We call on all national governments and international institutions to endorse and implement the framework. We urgently need a new global system for how we produce, distribute and consume food.

Food, fun and a life well lived

| Professor Matthew Gandy

| Department of Geography, UCL

Whenever I get to know a city there is a certain geography that I always replicate which consists of metro systems, bookshops and restaurants. I study the strange maps of new transport networks with intensity and enjoy those first tentative journeys to unknown reaches of an unfamiliar city.

As for bookshops I am drawn to esoteric treasure troves of second-hand books or the kind of specialist stores that have all the latest titles in their field. And then there are the restaurants: I am drawn to the kind of places that feel special in some indefinable way, to establishments that lie somewhat off the beaten track, to spaces that have become part of my mental image of the city through their associations with happy and unexpected memories.

I am about to have lunch in Paris. It is a glorious sunny day in May and I take the metro excitedly (and hungrily) to Saint-Germain-des-Prés. The restaurant I am heading for with a friend is a small Italian restaurant in a side street where the trendy sixth arrondissement meets the more upmarket seventh. The owners came from Sardinia eighteen years ago and have gradually built up a loyal clientele of mainly local people. Despite it being Monday lunchtime the restaurant quickly fills up and there is that unmistakable sound of multiple conversations with no background music: the mood is of itself and not electronically manipulated.

Our meal begins with antipasti lovingly arranged in circular formation like an edible clock: the strips of courgette and marinated peppers are delicious. For my main course I choose *filetti di rombo agli asparagi* [turbot filets with asparagus] and think of my brother-in-law who regularly goes sea fishing: a turbot is one of the most prized catches of all because of its flavour and also the skills needed to land such an elusive fish. As we wait expectantly I sip some of the house wine and admire the fresh peonies that adorn the table. The food arrives and is stupendous from the first mouthful. I realize that I am eating quite slowly to prolong the pleasure of the experience. My friend's choice of *penne a la Siciliana* consists of fresh pasta with an aubergine sauce that is quite extraordinary in its intensity. And then finally we share a *panna cotta* that is so light it almost floats off the plate.

Restaurants are an integral part of civic life: not public in the sense of libraries or parks, but nonetheless a space through which modern life is lived collectively. The cultural history of restaurants is inextricably tied with the history of cities as spaces for enjoyment, experimentation and self-fulfilment. The word restaurant, as the historian Rebecca Spang reminds us, is derived from the French word *restaurer* meaning not only to provide food but also to "restore" in the fullest sense[1]. As I step out into the Paris street I cannot help reflecting on Jürgen Habermas's recent return to the basic philosophical question of what the "good life" might consist of and how we might use the precious time that we have[2]. I wonder whether a modern philosophical conception of a "life well lived" might extend to a geography of fun in its culinary sense.

[1] Rebecca Spang, *The invention of the restaurant: Paris and modern gastronomy* (Cambridge, MA: Harvard University Press, 2000).

[2] Jürgen Habermas, "Are there post metaphysical answers to the question: what is the 'good life'?" trans. William Rehg in *The future of human nature* (Cambridge: Polity Press 2003 [2000]) pp. 1-15.

Food: the 'new' art in cities?

I **Regan Koch**

I Department of Geography, UCL

These are exciting times for food-loving urbanites. A popular explosion of new restaurants, events, markets and innovative dining concepts are pushing the boundaries of culinary culture and transforming urban landscapes.

The impact of these changes are such that scholar and critic Sharon Zukin has described food as 'the "new" art in the urban cultural experience[1]'. This is an intriguing proposition. It undeniably resonates with the sense of expression, experimentation and passion driving the contemporary enthusiasm for food. As with art, the host of adjectives used to describe current trends – foodie, gourmet, omnivore, street, exotic, artisan, absurd – fail to capture what ultimately must be sensed to be understood. Even more than art, the growth of food-based experiences present a (literal) re-orientation of cities toward destination and life-style based forms of consumption. If we accept the merit of the claim that 'food is the new art', a question that follows is whether this is something to be celebrated.

There are certainly reasons to be sceptical. Food tastes are, of course, cultural constructs. They inherently work as markers of distinction through which forms of elitism are produced and hierarchies maintained. Popular perceptions of food as a commodity to be experienced and entertained by – rather than sustained and nourished by – would seem to only perpetuate inequalities. A legitimate concern is that food can easily be appropriated as another tool of domination, leveraging urban space in favour of the more affluent. In a rush to follow the next food fad, difference can be reduced to matters of flavour while demand for premium quality food in some neighbourhoods can crowd out low-cost alternatives. Adorno and Horkheimer's critique of 'the culture industry perpetually cheat[ing] its consumers of what it perpetually promises' is perhaps given a new twist[2]. It is no longer the case that 'the diner must be satisfied with the menu', for in many cities prices are enough to keep some residents from even sitting down at the table.

There are many reasons, however, to be more optimistic. Just as the mass popularisation of art in cities expanded opportunities for exposure, there seems to be a growing awareness and appreciation of the importance of food in urban space. Farmers' markets are moving into the city like never before. Food festivals have become a ubiquitous component of urban leisure. Cooking

[1] Zukin S., *Naked City: The Death and Life of Authentic Urban Places.* Oxford University Press 2009.

[2] Adorno TW, Horkheimer M., *Dialectic of enlightenment.* Verso Books; 1997.

courses, demonstrations and tasting sessions regularly draw crowds. And just as postmodern aesthetic sensibilities challenged rigid distinctions between high and low forms of art, so too has the new enthusiasm for food brought about certain democratisations. One of these is, paradoxically, a more stringent and more embracing standard for what counts as 'good' food. At higher economic levels, food is increasingly expected to be locally produced, ethically sourced and environmentally sustainable. Independent, local and small-scale ventures are often more adept at meeting these criteria, presenting a challenge to the mass production so often implicated in the darker sides of the food industry. At the lower-

end, divergent practices are helping to shift consumer expectations of value from quantity to quality. A diverse range of ethnic foods are celebrated for their authenticity. Mobile vendors and 'street food' are gaining culinary approval that enhances their social benefits entry-level economic opportunities. Collective actions are highlighting limited access to healthy food as a social injustice. In response, many inhabitants are digging up plots, forming co-ops and growing their own. Supermarkets, restaurants and fast food outlets are having to raise their game to stay competitive at all levels.

If food is the new art, the prevailing aesthetic seems to be that good food

needs to have a good story. If its origins
can be narrated, its credentials clarified,
its meaning or value articulated, then
it can satisfy the emergent criteria. The
increasing conversation and evaluation
surrounding food points to another feature of these developments. Food as an
urban experience is generating all sorts
of novel ways for people to come together to eat, to socialise, and to collectively
share in the pleasures of being together
in cities. Given that food is of course
much more than art, these developments demand our attention. Certainly
they open up new spaces for pleasure
and politics, for imagining more satiat-
ing and more equitable futures.

Foodcycling

I Lara Glass
I FoodCycle

The problem: 400,000 tonnes of surplus food are wasted every year; 4 million people are affected by food poverty in the UK; and over 2.4 million people in the UK are currently searching for work.

An organisation called FoodCycle is tackling this by combining surplus food with volunteers and a free kitchen space to create nutritious meals and positive social change in the community.

In late September 2010, seven project leaders found an unused kitchen space, supermarkets eager to be involved in reducing their land-fill footprint, and a group of volunteers. This was the formula needed for cooking to begin in the Bromley-by-Bow Centre every Sunday lunchtime.

Mexican West Coast peppers:

Ingredients:
5 tablespoons olive oil
300g/10oz *tempeh* (or potato), cut into 1cm cubes
2 red onions, thinly sliced
4 garlic cloves, sliced
2 red chillies, chopped
2 tablespoons coriander seeds, crushed
5 peppers (2 red, 2 yellow and 1 green), deseeded and sliced
350g/12oz cooked pinto beans
24 black olives, stoned and halved
Soy sauce
Large handful of coriander leaves, chopped

To make:
Heat half the oil in a large pan and when hot, fry the *tempeh* (or potatoes) until brown. Remove from pan and set aside.
Add the remaining oil to the pan and when hot, fry the onion until it starts to soften. Add the garlic, chilli and crushed coriander seeds. Fry for a couple of minutes.
Add the peppers and fry, stirring regularly, until they start to soften. Add the pinto beans and olives. When the beans are heated through, add the *tempeh* to pan and stir well.
Add soy sauce to taste and the chopped coriander.
Serve immediately with fresh fruit salsa and rice.

The outcome: a free, nutritious, recycled meal and the sparks of community spirit being built. Since then, we have cooked for about 30 people each week.

The kitchen is energised with chopping, peeling, frying and sizzling – all produced with food that would have landed on the dump because the packaging wasn't sealed, or the product had passed its sell-by date. We prove this fresh produce can make delicious vegetarian meals and through our meals are raising awareness of the waste that is unnecessary.

This isn't just about providing a café service to the people we cook for. It's about creating a welcoming social environment that people enjoy coming to each week as much as it is about providing nutritious food and reducing food waste. What's more, a tradition has sprung up of reading poetry over pudding. The project is developing into something that is valued by a large number of the local community.

Not only has the Sunday lunch shaped new friendships, but beneficiaries are being empowered through their involvement in preparing, cooking, serving and clearing while working together to produce a creative meal from a mix of vegetables and fruit.

From tea to *Tao*

I **Shun Long**
I Cha-Tao Research Society

To enter the *Tao* through tea is an important indicator that human civilisation is going to enter the fourth dimension from the third dimension. It is an unprecedented fortune for human beings!

Human civilisation has evolved four different ways of governing. Two of these ways are more extroverted – using logic and force to win people over – and two are more introverted, using empathy and self-awareness to govern groups of people. The Chinese politician and statesman Guan Zhong (c. 720-645 BC) described these four ways of governing as follows:

1. To govern the general public by the way of reasoning is called *Wang Dao* (kingly way).
2. To govern the general public with armed force is called *Pao Dao* (dictatorial way).
3. To govern the general public with affection is called *Dee Dao* (royal way).

However, referring to the fourth way of governing, Guan Zhong commented that the first three ways of governance have written records, whereas the fourth way of governance has no historical record. This was because it could not be described in words. With this kind of governance, everyone communicates with each other using their mind but without speaking words. Everyone's lifestyle is very simple so that each person's life and their relationship with the natural world can have a high degree of harmony. This kind of governance is part of the internal management of civilians, with each civilian acting as the ruler. There is an ancient Chinese book called *Shung Shu*. It describes this particular state of governance, where everyone communicates with god, heaven and earth; where all the leaders of small or large populations have advanced wisdom and love to be able to "gather nine clans together in peace".

Unfortunately, almost three thousand years since Guan Zhong's writings, Chinese history has been such that people have gone the opposite way and become too self-satisfied. Many dynasties have risen and fallen, all of them adopting the way of "executing nine clans" rather than living in peace.

In this respect, it can be said that over the last three thousand years, the Chinese people have regressed. However, such regression is also an opportunity for a return to a simplicity and a kind of 'civilisation upgrade'.

The Mayan prophecy about a cataclysmic event on December 21, 2012, has led to many speculations about the evolution of humans after 2012 and the emergence of a new civilisation. The emergence of any new civilisation must be accompanied by the following major changes in human activity:

1. Emergence of energy-based medicine: Ancient China and India understood the energy system of the human body more than many other nations. In recent years, Germany has also made significant innovations in this field.

2. Changes of education: more Masters and PhD degrees will mean more complex knowledge, which may result in difficulty solving problems with simple solutions. People need to model themselves on the simplicity of the way three-year old children use their heart and brain to understand the sort of education we need.

3. Changes in agriculture and food: the world's governments need to understand that only by improving the quality and quantity of food production per unit area, and making it more sustainable, can we protect the environment from catastrophe. By doing this we can also improve the health of global populations and the financial burden of medical expenses.

4. Changes of political economy: the way of governance must find a way of emphasising the need for spiritual communication – the main principle of the fourth dimension, instead of focusing on the notion of elected politicians.

5. Change of lifestyle: humans will need to return to a lifestyle which is simple, natural, and fearless. They will be able to experience the realm of spirituality that is "from tea to *Tao*". Eventually a lifestyle able to "gather nine clans together in peace" will be truly manifested in Taiwan.

In Taiwan, a world-class sculptor recently carved a block of wood into a square cage with a person trapped inside. The implication of this artwork was that square cubes are created by humans, whereas only rounded edges and curves exist in the natural world. Humans use their minds to create unnatural square cages and trap themselves inside them. We look forward to seeing our old civilisation taken over by a new civilisation after 2012. Human beings will hopefully be able to develop their society to incorporate both spiritual and material elements. You are invited to join this revolution.

Fruit carving

I Sumalee Murphy

My name is Sumalee and I grew up in the tiny farming village of Rachasan, in Chacheongsao province of Thailand, two hours east of Bangkok.

In my country village life is very different from that of the big city, especially when you think of how the city has developed today. When I was growing up it seemed like the country was a land of calm and peace, with Buddhism at its heart.

The people of the countryside were far from rich, but they did not need much for their straightforward lives. If the rice crops failed, there was always faith in the great and respected Buddha to give us hope for the next harvest.

Some people in the village kept chickens, but to see red meat on the table was very unusual. We were content to eat a simple meal of rice accompanied mainly by vegetables. This was the way we knew and we were grateful to have enough to fill our stomachs. The fields and the small areas of fruiting trees planted in the village provided all our needs.

Since we were close to nature we were happy to use its benefits in very many different ways. Fruits and vegetables were carved into beautiful decorative shapes both to act as containers and generally to brighten the appearance of a meal. Flowers were fashioned into garlands and beautiful displays to enhance any village ceremony – especially at the temple of the Buddha – which marked all phases of village life.

Even the banana tree was pressed into service. As well as its fruits, the flowers were eaten, the thick stalks carved for funeral ceremonies, and the giant leaves shaped, folded and finally sewn to provide trays for food or containers for cooking.

The balance seemed right: we used simply what nature provided.

My formal training in carving was scanty, but since moving to the UK, I have developed a real enthusiasm for carving skills (which are said to have originated in the royal palaces of Thailand) and am doing whatever I can to pass on my knowledge so that yesterday's wonderful crafts are not lost to the world.

For me carving fruit and vegetables not only creates a close link to my village background but works as a sort of meditation. When I am carving my thoughts concentrate on the piece of nature I am reshaping, and any worries or fears I might have fade far into the background.

I gain immense satisfaction from knowing that the beautiful piece of work I am creating is a product of a tradition that has been passed down over dozens of Thai generations using the same natural fruits and vegetables that were at hand in the village. My husband and daughter aren't so happy that the cooking hasn't been done ... but that's another story!

Global Generation change

I Jane Riddiford

I Global Generation

Thursday June 2nd, 2011. I excitedly open the email that lands in my inbox. It is from Stephen England, one of the chefs from Baxter Story who provide the catering for the *Guardian*'s in-house restaurant.

He has sent me a photograph and recipe of the meal they have created out of the produce delivered by Global Generation's young gardeners the day before.

The story behind the meal is why we often refer to our work as a process of growing food, growing people and growing relationships between people. Our work is about providing opportunities for young people to develop their potential so they can become catalysts for positive change in their local area. Growing vegetables on an unused section of a large development site in the middle of King's Cross, London, and selling them to nearby restaurants is a doorway into another way of being; a ticket into another world for many of the young people we work with.

Walking into the garden today felt like a different country. The smell of the chives made me think that hard work definitely pays off. Watching the radishes and the peas grow big and

tall really made an impact on me. I never realised that nature could make me change in so many different ways. I used to think gardening would be boring but it's been really fun and it's given me an insight into business. I like sharing our knowledge of how things grow with the chefs. This experience makes me want to take another path, I used to be on the bad way but now I want to help other people so they can have the same feeling you have given me.

Participant, 14 years old.

Collecting food waste from the restaurants and feeding it to the worms really got me thinking about that saying 'one man's waste is another man's treasure'. It sure did get me thinking, and now I acknowledge all the luxuries that I have.

Participant, 14 years old.

As these young people learn to become ambassadors for the best part of themselves, they are having a small but positive effect on the businesses that are moving into King's Cross.

Wherever possible we try to structure activities so that our participants can learn about their complete selves. In our work, this includes three territories of experience, which we refer to as 'I, We and The Planet.' 'I' represents a deeper and different sense of self which is without boundaries and common to all. 'We' represents the power and potential in relationships to bring about change

Guardian's 'Global Generation' salad:

Ingredients:

Spring radishes (washed) - 1 bunch
Egg noodles (cooked)– 200g
Cucumber – roughly a quarter
Coriander root chopped – 1 tsp
Pea cress shoots – a few
Coriander sprigs – a few
Sesame seeds (toasted) - 1 tsp
Soy sauce – 1 tsp
Sesame oil – 1 dessert spoon
Red wine vinegar - 1 tsp
Garlic purée – quarter of a tsp
Seasoning

To make:

Cut the radishes into a variety of shapes (halves, quarters and slices)
De-seed the cucumber and cut into 5mm slices on the bias
Whisk the soy, garlic, sesame and red wine vinegar together to make the dressing
Cut through the cooked noodles with a pair of kitchen scissors to make it easier to serve.
Use your hands to toss the noodles, cucumber, radish and chopped coriander together.
Add the dressing and seasoning then lightly toss once again.
Place the salad into a serving bowl and scatter the coriander sprigs and pea shoots over the salad.
Finally sprinkle the toasted sesame seeds over the salad.

and the energy that emerges from bringing different people together. 'The Planet' represents using both man-made and natural resources to support the planet and make a positive impact.

Time and again we have observed that when the understanding of who we really are and what we are a part of develops, there is a spirit of openness, connectedness and a willingness to embrace new things. Which is why we call our organisation 'Global Generation'; it is all about growing a body of young people who are the generators for a new kind of 'global' awareness out of which a new story for the future is growing.

NATURE

CORPORATE LIFE

COMMON GROUND

CITY

A UNIQUE SPACE FOR PEOPLE TO CONNECT

URBAN YOUTH

IGNITING NEW CONVERSATIONS

Good food for everyone forever

| Colin Tudge
| Campaign for Real Farming

We're told that if we're to feed the human species over the next few decades and into the future then we must either learn to love industrial agriculture, with high-tech, hyper-productive monocultures, or tighten our belts and learn to live on lentils.

Otherwise there just won't be enough – certainly not to feed the 9.5 billion who are likely to be with us by 2050.

So the high-tech zealots are breeding sows that produce 30 piglets a year; and chickens that reach slaughter weight in five weeks; and cows that give up to 15,000 litres of milk in a year – more than ten times what a wild cow would give; and clones – genetic replicas of the most productive animals; and GM soya and maize and wheat to feed them all on; and turning out tonnes and tonnes of fertilizer to feed the crops, and pesticide to protect them; all of it deemed necessary just to keep pace; and all of it wonderfully appealing to the stock market. The vegetarians, on the other hand, say that to eat any meat at all is not only morally bad but is downright destructive, and will soon be impossible if we really want to feed everybody, because livestock takes too much resource.

Both prospects look grim – though my sympathies lie with the vegetarians rather than the industrialists who, if they continue on their present course, will surely kill us all. But in either case, the basic argument is nonsense. We don't need high tech and clones and GM crops and monocultures and lashings of industrial chemistry, but neither must we tighten our belts. We could easily produce plenty of food for everybody – and the food could and should be of the highest standard, scaling the heights of the world's great cuisines. We should eat less meat in the future than present-day Brits and Americans do – but we certainly don't need to be vegetarians. In fact, all we really need to do is to re-learn how to cook – the most vital of all skills, which successive British governments have done their best to kill off over the past half century, to make way for food processing with all its ostensible profits. If we grew food properly, and cooked it properly, we could all live very well indeed, forever. In truth, "The future belongs to the gourmet".

On the technophile front, Britain's government Chief Scientific Adviser Sir John Beddington has been telling us of late that we need to increase total food output by 50% by 2050 just to keep pace with rising numbers and aspiration[1].

[1] The "Foresight report": The Future of Food and Farming, challenges and choices for global sustainability. (http://tinyurl.com/ForesightReport2011).

In the starkest possible contrast, Hans Herren, co-chair of the IAASTD (International Assessment of Agricultural Knowledge, Science, and Technology for Development) tells us that we already produce enough to feed 14 billion people. It doesn't look that way, because so much of what's produced is wasted, one way and another. The key difference between the two is that Hans Herren is an agriculturalist, who has spent his life in farming, and John Beddington is not. Like most recent British scientific advisers and secretaries of state, Professor Beddington is new to the subject.

Still you may feel – so what? If human numbers go on rising then we will soon get to 14 billion – and then what? But the same UN demographers who tell us that the population will reach 9.5 billion by 2050 also tell us that numbers are leveling out – so there should never be more than 9.5 billion. So we don't really need more than we produce already. We just need to produce it more sustainably – with less collateral damage.

Why do we waste so much of the food we produce? Well, a huge amount is spoiled. In the third world up to a half can be lost to fungi and insects and so on between harvest and the kitchen. In rich countries, about a third is thrown away after it reaches the kitchen. But in addition, in the frenetic desire to produce as much meat as possible as quickly as possible (in the interests purely of money) we now feed about half the world's cereals to livestock – cere-

als we could perfectly well be eating ourselves.

Ah, you might say, but if we didn't give all that cereal to livestock, wouldn't that condemn us (if condemn is the right word) to a vegan diet? Not at all. First, cereals cannot sensibly be grown just anywhere. On steep slopes, and in wetland or wherever it rains a lot, or in semi-deserts, and woodland the world over, cereals can be impossible to grow or more trouble than they are worth – and that's where we can raise cattle and sheep. Britain has loads of excellent grassland, largely though not exclusively on the uplands. Whenever we grow food crops for our own consumption there are always some that don't quite come up to scratch and often there are surpluses, while even the best-run kitchens produce leftovers – and these provide the provender for pigs and poultry.

Of course, if we want to produce the most protein, energy, and other nutrients on the land available then we must focus first on plants – but we will always make best use of the available land (and water and so on) if we incorporate some animals into the farming landscape. So if we set out to grow food as if we really wanted to feed people without too much damage to the rest (as opposed to growing food to make the most money possible without regard to the rest) then we would certainly focus on plants, but we would also produce some animals – and the output would be very mixed because combinations of plants and animals make most use of the resources. So we'd have "plenty of plants, not much meat, and maximum variety" – and these nine words summarise the best of the nutritional theory of the past half century. In short: farming that is designed to provide us with enough (without wrecking the rest) also provides us with the best possible nutrition. A great serendipity.

But also – and this is the second great serendipity, and the point of this article – "plenty of plants, not much meat, and maximum variety" – is the basis of all the world's greatest traditional cuisines. The great cuisines worldwide make admirable use of tripes of all kinds (tripe and white beans in Siena is among my fondest gastro memories), and pigs' heads and trotters (which are now in vogue and sell for £5.00 a go in Borough market in London). Indian and Chinese cooking, both without peer, are extrapolations of rice and wheat. (I could be a vegetarian if I could live in Kerala, living on *dosas* and *idlis*). North European cooking, not least in Britain, was wonderfully tasty – but also economical. It is impossible to improve on lamb stew made with scrag end, with dumplings (and carrots and turnips).

This, above all, is what we must re-discover: the sheer glory of traditional cooking, evolved in literally millions of kitchens by people at large over literally thousands of years, and occasionally extrapolated by outstanding chefs into *haute cuisine*.

Match serious cooking to farming that is actually designed to feed people and our problems all but disappear. We, human beings, could be looking forward with reasonable optimism to the next million years. Or else, if we carry on as we are, led by "experts" who in truth are seriously ill-informed or prefer to ignore the obvious, and are driven by an economy geared only to the maximisation and the concentration of wealth, we will be lucky to get through the next century.

Growing a healthy revolution

| Anthony Stonehouse
| Development Planning Unit, UCL

We cannot talk about achieving food security without talking about the public health fallout of food insecurity and the spatial distribution of healthy, affordable food in the city.

Milwaukee, Wisconsin, in the United States is a case in point: with approximately 9.5% of Milwaukee County's population diagnosed with diabetes[1], an obesity rate of 30.2%[2], and physical inactivity at 25.5%[3], access to healthy, affordable food is a major issue for Milwaukee's urban poor. 'Food desert' is a term that describes "areas where low-income residents of colour do not have access to healthy and affordable food and fast food restaurants dominate the landscape[4]." According to the 2010 Milwaukee Health Report, the conclusion may be drawn that based on where someone lives in Milwaukee, they would have better or worse access to healthy food, and that the worst access to healthy food is located in the areas with the highest population density, the lowest incomes, the lowest education level, and the largest Black population in the city[5]. Food deserts are breeding food insecurity in urban communities across the U.S., and this in turn can lead to psychological issues such as stress and depression resulting in physical inactivity and obesity[6].

Founded in 1995, Growing Power (GP), in Milwaukee, is a non-profit urban agriculture training centre focused on building community food security. GP challenges the current global food system through the use of innovative urban agriculture systems which focus on the reuse, recycling, and reclamation of natural inputs like water and organic waste. In addition, GP has been working to build diverse and resilient social networks, not only in Milwaukee, but regionally, nationally, and even internationally.

Will Allen, the founder and CEO of GP, speaks of the "Good Food Revolution", a term that he uses to describe increasing access to locally grown, healthy foods for marginalised communities and launching an attack against the current global food system. The Good Food Revolution focuses on bringing communities together to think about and work collectively towards solutions. Unlike other movements, it is not tied to strict dogma. Will Allen acknowledges he is not a food purist, but he is encouraging people to eat and live better with what they have available to them and work towards changing those options. The Good Food Revolution is open to everyone and the involvement of parents and children is the backbone of the movement.

Engaging with youth and incorporating agro-ecology into the educational system in the U.S. is crucial to the success of GP's vision of building local sustainable food systems. Will Allen states that this challenge begins even prior to birth with pre-natal nutrition as well as what children are fed at day-care centers, kindergarten, and all through school.

Partnerships are key to the success of GP. Through the Farm Fresh to Milwaukee Public Schools (MPS) Program and other farm-to-school initiatives, the organisation aims to deliver locally-grown produce to Milwaukee schoolchildren who have little access to healthy food as well as designing and delivering a curriculum focusing on the biological, ecological, and economic advantages of urban agriculture[7.] In addition to these connections, GP is working with corporations such as Kohl's, creating vegetable gardens around the parking lot of its corporate offices. During the summer the gardens function as a teaching tool for the children at the day care center and the bulk of the harvest is donated to a local food pantry. On the global scale, GP is working with food security specialists from Uganda and Kenya as part of the Bold Food Fellows exchange project to examine food insecurity issues and urban agriculture techniques to improve food productivity in urban areas. These partnerships are connecting communities with local resources with the aim of increasing awareness of food insecurity and improving local capacities for growing and accessing healthy and affordable food in the city.

By involving children and focusing on their need for healthy food, GP is ensuring the next generation of good food revolutionaries. When people see that they can grow their own food, and it can improve their health and nutrition, and it is more affordable than what they are buying at the stores, they are more likely to believe in it and tell others about it.

[1] Centers for Disease Control and Prevention. 2008a. County Level Estimates of Diagnosed Diabetes: 2008 Estimates of the Percentage of Adults with Diagnosed Diabetes in Wisconsin. Available: http://tinyurl.com/6434paa [Accessed 19 April, 2011].

[2] Centers for Disease Control and Prevention. 2008c. County Level Estimates of Obesity: 2008 Estimates of the Percentage of Adults Who Are Obese in Wisconsin. Available: http://tinyurl.com/6434paa.

[3] Centers for Disease Control and Prevention. 2008b. County Level Estimates of Leisure-Time Physical Inactivity: 2008 Estimates of the Percentage of Adults Who Are Physically Inactive in Wisconsin. Available: http://apps.nccd.cdc.gov/DDT_STRS2/CountyPrevalenceData.aspx?mode=DBT.

[4] Mari Gallagher Research and Consulting Group. 2006. Good Food: Examining the Impact of Food Deserts on Public Health in Chicago Available: www.marigallagher.com.

[5] Chen, H.Y. et al. 2010. *Milwaukee Health Report 2010: Health Disparities in Milwaukee by Socioeconomic Status*. Milwaukee, WI: Center for Urban Population Health.

[6] Dinour, L.M. et al. 2007. The Food Insecurity-Obesity Paradox: A Review of the Literature and the Role Food Stamps May Play. *Journal of the American Dietetic Association*, 107, 1952-1961.

[7] HERZOG, K. 2009. Growing Power wins grant to help feed MPS students Journal Sentinel [Online]. Available: http://www.jsonline.com/blogs/lifestyle/79455972.html# [Accessed 8 April, 2011].

Growing a multicultural community garden

I **Mila Campoy**
I Calthorpe Project

The Calthorpe Project is a community garden in King's Cross, Central London. It was created in 1984 when local people campaigned to preserve the site as a green space against the council plan of selling the land for development. Since then the garden has become an important part of the local community.

The 1.2 acre garden is used by people of all ages and ethnic backgrounds for a range of activities. The Project offers programmes for children, adults and numerous community classes, as well as a place to relax, eat, socialise and play sports. The site also includes a space where local people can grow their own food.

Food growing, and the related activities of cooking and eating, play an important role in the life of the Project. Food growing is something that any age and ability can do and, in addition, it creates an almost instant feeling of wellbeing. There is something about planting, watering and harvesting that connects us with our primal selves and acts as a powerful therapeutic activity.

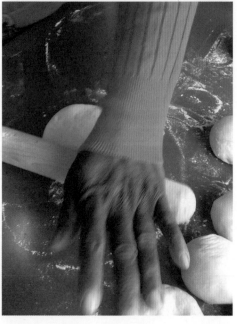

Although food growing has been a key element of the activities of all community gardens, we have noticed an increase of interest in the past few years. We have redeveloped and amplified our growing area to accommodate this increasing demand. There are three main areas for food growing at the Project: the Bangladeshi women's group's allotment, the family allotments and a communal growing area.

The Bangladeshi women's group allotment was formed by 18 older women and each one has her own plot. They all come from an agricultural background but currently live in flats and miss their contact with the land. For them, it is very important to be able to grow herbs and vegetables from their native country in the heart of the city. They visit the allotment daily to tend the plots and incorporate some of what they have grown into their family cooking. Their work on the allotment allows them to be in contact with other women and helps them to integrate with the rest of the community. As a result of this women's group allotment, the women feel more confident about participating in the community. They have cooked at some of our events and festivals and teach people how to cook some of their traditional dishes.

The family allotments were created five years ago with the purpose of encouraging families to eat more healthy diets. Presently they are used by a combination of families and single older people.

Although the users don't act as a group, they interact with others in the garden. We support them with tools, seeds, physical help and advice and further-more, try to empower them by encour-aging them to use this space as their own garden.

The communal growing area is a large area with seven raised beds, one green-house, two polytunnels and a compost scheme. It is linked to a wildlife area, which includes a pond that is impor-tant both as an educational tool and to support our organic methods. Once a week we have gardening sessions with children under five years old. They learn about the seasons and how plants go from seed to flower to fruit to the plate. They also learn about what vegetables look and taste like. We also run activi-ties for 8 to 12-year-old children. They have their own plot and help out with the seasonal tasks of watering, digging and harvesting. This participation helps them learn about gardening and nature, and about where their food comes from.

Once a week, and in partnership with RSVP (an organisation offering the retired and senior people the opportu-nity to volunteer), we work with a group of around 20 older people. The group is very committed to the weekly sessions and because of their large number and their dedication, they do the lion's share of work in the growing area. They are highly valued members of the Project.

Many of these older people are migrants from South America who came to live and work in this country many years ago. They have raised their families and are now on their own at home. Although they socialise and live active lives, they are, at times, a little isolated. The food growing project has had a huge impact on their lives: they do physical exercise, have a chance to socialise and learn new skills. We share lunch together and people bring food they have prepared at home. By learning to use new veg-etables, people improve their diet and recover the motivation to cook more food themselves.

In addition, we organise events and festivals focused on food and workshops in making jams, pickles and preserves, using our own products whenever pos-sible. For example, during the Apple Day Festival, we take the community to an apple orchard in Hampstead and then prepare a day full of apple games and competitions. We have also recently begun selling products to the People's Supermarket and a local restaurant, the Lumen café. This means we now grow food in a community garden with people from the community and sell it in the community.

Pesto kale:

We started to experiment with kale two years ago and were surprised by discovering the different varieties, its fantastic versatility and its ability to grow – and be harvested – all year round.

We tried every single dish you can imagine: kale omelette, kale soup, fried kale with garlic and spices; we added it to stir fries, salads, broths, rice, and much more, but our favourite recipe is pesto kale.

Ingredients:

100g kale
2 handful of basil leaves
1 handful of pine nuts
A pinch of salt
3 tsp of olive oil
Grated parmesan cheese to taste

To make:

Take out the central stem of the leaf and finely chop the rest. Boil the leaves for 5 minutes. Drain off the water. Mix with the rest of the ingredients and blend until you've made a smooth paste.
You can add this sauce to pasta, potatoes, salads or eat just with bread. It is delicious.

Growing Communities

I Michael Roberts Jr.

I Development Planning Unit, UCL

Growing Communities (GC) has taken on the entire food economy.

Urban farms make food growing an important and viable use of space in the city, educating the public and providing an outlet for healthier lifestyles. Farmers' markets make healthy local ingredients more visible and accessible. Community Supported Agriculture (CSA), through a direct link between producer and consumer, can ensure a regular supply of better food for the consumer and a guaranteed market for the farmer. GC has taken all of these ingredients for a better food system and makes them accessible to the people that have the most impact on the whole system: the end consumer.

GC began as Northeast London CSA in 1993 to serve thirty families. Initially, the group partnered with a farm in Buckinghamshire, approximately forty-five miles from London, to provide a weekly offering of fruits and vegetables to its members. The aim was to promote an alternative to supermarkets, packaged foods, and the massive, anonymous supply chains that characterise today's unsustainable food system.

Weekend working trips to the supplying farms inspired members to begin cultivating within the city. In 1996, they began with a small space in Clissold Park. Since then, GC's urban cultivation has evolved to include three market gardens across Hackney and a steadily increasing number of "micro-sites." Combined, these sites cover only 0.2 hectares, but provide the heart of GC's activities.

Unlike traditional CSA, which provides members with produce from a single farm or a local cooperative, the GC box scheme pulls together a range of goods from the ultra-local to imported internationally. Members choose the size and content (veg-only or fruit-only) of their boxes and pick them up at sites around Hackney. GC's own production sites provide a small but vital contribution to the scheme. In 2009, the market gardens generated 300 salad bags a week at their peak. Not only does local production guarantee the freshest possible salad greens, it also gives members a tangible example of how their buying habits can make an impact.

GC takes the important step of placing local food in context with its "Food Zone" model, which determines priorities for its box scheme and is central to their proposition for a better food economy[1]. The main conviction behind the Food Zone model is that food should be grown as close to the city as possible, but some products are more appropriately sourced farther afield. For instance, salad greens and strawberries are very labour intensive and benefit from short transport distances. Orchards, on the other hand, are better

[1] Growing Communities, "Manifesto for Feeding Cities." (http://tinyurl.com/foodzones /)

suited for lands at the edge of the city, while grains or other more intensive field crops are best grown in the rural hinterlands. So long as attention is still given to appropriate scale, fair trading practices, and ecological growing methods, the Food Zone Model places urban growing at the heart of a viable food economy, connecting local urban and peri-urban growers and the broader food system at large.

With nearly 600 subscribers to date, the scheme provides more than just a regular supply of fresh and sustainable food. Regular subscription to a box scheme gives membership in GC and a say in how the scheme is administered. Even casual consumers are kept abreast of goings-on through a regular newsletter and updates on the organisation. In addition, there are scads of delicious recipes for the inevitable moment of "I have too many beetroots and I need to do something creative with them."

The Stoke Newington Farmers' Market, which GC began in 2003, offers another outlet to connect citizens with their food. Farmers and food producers come from as far as 129 miles from the market (though the majority come from much closer) and provide only goods that are Soil Association certified organic. As the first farmer's market in London to accept Healthy Start vouchers, the Stoke Newington Farmers' Market has made local healthy food accessible to all members of the community.

The success of the box scheme and the Stoke Newington Farmers' Market allowed GC to make an important decision that faces all like organisations. In 2005, GC made the transition from dependence on donor and grant funding to financial self-sufficiency. While the majority of income comes from the farmers' market and box schemes, this transition also required a shift in focus from education and outreach to more intensive production.

The more profitable market activities have so far served to subsidise its market garden operations, but urban cultivation remains a critical ingredient to the overall programme. The market gardens continue to see a constant flow of volunteers and visitors, proving that economic viability need not interfere with community outreach.

In fact, GC has continued to expand on its model for local food production and community-led trading through its Urban Apprenticeship, Patchwork Farm, and Start-up programmes. The apprenticeship gives prospective farmers the necessary training in food production, marketing and administration, while the Patchwork programme seeks new spaces in the city for these apprentices to cultivate. Meanwhile, new community trading schemes have popped up around Greater London with the support of GC's Start-up programme.

By starting small and organising around demand, GC has insured that each progressive step it makes bolsters the relationships necessary to create a sustainable food system. Whether stopping at the farmers' market, picking up a veg box from down the street, or digging in and lending a hand with the market gardens, the vision for a better food system is apparent. Piecemeal, each ingredient may bring some benefit to the way we grow, sell, or eat – but in putting them together Growing Communities offers a recipe for better consumption, and ultimately a better food economy.

Harvesting fruit in the city

| Michael Stuart

| Kensal to Kilburn Fruit Harvesters

As a child I knew the best blackberry patches in suburban Stanmore, London, where I lived. I spent summer afternoons picking blackberries to take home in stained, dripping plastic bags for my mother to turn into apple and blackberry pies.

I was still blackberrying in my forties, although now living in Kilburn. I was struck afresh by the apples and pears that fall to the ground and rot in so many peoples' gardens. Why not pick them? I felt too embarrassed to knock on a stranger's door and ask. I was sure most people would say no. But a group with a name would give an air of legitimacy and open doors. So, Kensal to Kilburn Fruit Harvesters was born.

I started by putting up leaflets in local shops and community centres and soon came across a couple of people who liked the idea and helped with planning. Two years on, 110 people volunteer to pick, 50 people offer their trees and we've had to turn gardens away and stop publicising the project. The local media love us. The local council is a fan and provides some modest funding. As the library manager said when he agreed to lend out our telescopic harvesting tools "What's not to like?"

Avoiding waste is our main motivation. We've picked 2.5 tons of fruit in two seasons and are scratching the surface in a quarter of one borough, Brent. I estimate there may be over 3.5 million kilograms of fallen fruit in London. This is another instance to add to the estimated 18% of purchased food thrown away in the UK.

Baked apple:

A simple, quick recipe that uses cupboard ingredients. Ideal for when you're already using the oven.

Ingredients:

Apples
Sugar
Butter
Dried fruits
Nuts
Spices (e.g. cinnamon)

To make:

Core the apples and score a line around the waist so they don't explode in the oven. Then stuff with any combination of whichever of these you fancy: sugar, butter, dried fruit, nuts, cinnamon.

Place on a baking tray or dish and bake at 180 C for between 30 minutes to an hour.

Serve as they are or with cream or custard.

In some cases, we've harvested apples in a back garden while the owners were bringing supermarket apples through the front door, unaware of their own ripe produce. One man stopped his car, got out and asked if it was true you had to inject trees so the apples weren't poisonous! We Londoners have out-sourced our hunter-gatherer skills to supermarkets and lost self-confidence in the process.

The plethora of old fruit trees in local gardens show that 50 years ago it was very different. People valued fruit trees enough to wait many years, until they bore fruit.

Fruit gathering re-connects people to food as a natural product. In the push and pull of global-local it brings food production into almost every street. The project has made me much more aware of my surroundings and the edible plants that are all around. I can now go for walk and almost any-where in London, I can find something edible growing.

One reason people don't harvest their trees is there's too much for them to eat. In looking for places to distribute fruit we create new local connections with neighbours as we help each other, not only with the harvest, but also with other local projects. Our favourite project is a homeless charity where clients bake apple pies at a mosque to fundraise for Pakistan flood relief. These clients enjoyed the feeling of helping

others for a change. There's also more scope to work with schools, link with youth and older people's groups, artists and local jam and chutney makers.

We have our limits. We harvest each tree in one go sometimes, waiting until a third of the fruit has fallen to make sure what's left is really ripe. If we could make several visits, we could pick each fruit when it's individually ripe and there'd be even less waste. We also need to find ways to share the organising work, which is the least popular part and tends to fall on one or two people, creating a bottleneck. And we are not economically competitive with mass-produced fruit. If we costed the time taken to organise, pick and distribute our 2.5 tons of fruit we'd make a financial loss even though the fruit is free.

But the potential is truly significant. In London alone there may be 3 million kilogramme of wasted fruit growing in back gardens. Nationally, there are dozens of similar projects – many of which are known as 'Abundance Projects' – and I'd love to see the whole country covered. A small central organisation promoting the concept and sharing good practice could help speed up what is spreading by word of mouth. In the meantime the best advice for anyone wanting to start a harvesting group is to google 'Sheffield Abundance' and to go for it.

Himalayan meals

| Professor Anthony Costello
| UCL Institute for Global Health

In 1984, when Helen and I arrived, after a two day soaking monsoon trek involving fording countless terrifyingly swollen streams, in a small rural district of Nepal where I had gone for a two year residency as a medical officer, my biggest fear was the diet.

I had heard about *daal-bhaat-tarkari* (boiled rice accompanied by lentil soup and seasonal vegetables) and it sounded acceptably nutritious, but tourists had casually warned me it was dull and tasteless. The idea of eating platters of rice and lentils twice a day for two years did not sound like fun.

The small middle-hill town of Baglung sits on a plateau above an escarpment leading down to the Kali Gandaki river, which steams down the deepest gorge on earth between the Himalayan peaks of Dhaulagiri and Annapurna. Above the town bazaar, the hills are terraced with rice paddies and fields of *makai* (maize) and *daal* (lentils) bordered by bamboo clusters, banana plants and marijuana bushes.

In villages there is a joint family system where parents and married sons and their families live together in decorated wood and dried mud houses. Almost every family, apart from a few wealthy Newari shopkeepers in the town bazaar, lives off the food grown from their own land. Meals are communal, and the family sit cross-legged on mats on the kitchen floor, eating from flat, compart-mentalised aluminium trays, or from plates with accompanying bowls. To begin the meal a small amount of food is offered to the Gods. The elders and men are served first, by wives or daughters-in-law, and the food is eaten with the right hand following a ritual ablution to wash the hands, rinse the mouth and gargle. All food is served at the same

Daal and achaar:

Here is a recipe for a favourite *daal* and the accompanying tomato and onion pickle, courtesy of Jyoti Pathak.

Ingredients:

1 cup red lentils
2 large cloves garlic
2 teaspoons of minced fresh ginger
½ teaspoon salt
½ teaspoon ground turmeric
¼ teaspoon ground cumin
¼ teaspoon ground coriander
3 tablespoons clarified butter
1 to 2 dried red chillies
½ teaspoon cumin seeds
A small pinch of asafetida
1 tablespoon fresh lemon or lime juice
¼ cup chopped fresh coriander leaves
2-3 finely chopped small onions
½ cup chopped tomatoes.

To make:

Wash the lentils. Mix them with garlic, ginger, salt, turmeric, ground cumin and coriander, 1 tablespoon of clarified butter and 3 ½ cups of water in large pot. Bring to the boil uncovered and stirring occasionally. Do not skim the foam. Reduce heat to low and simmer for 25 minutes.

Separately heat the remaining butter until sizzling, add the chillies and cumin seeds for 10 seconds, sprinkle in the asafetida, and immediately pour into the daal in the saucepan and stir. Mix in the lemon or lime juice and serve with a covering of tomato, fresh coriander leaves and sliced onions.

For the *achaar* chop 3 medium tomatoes, 4 small fresh chillies, ¼ cup of chopped fresh coriander leaves, 1 clove of garlic, 1 tsp of chopped fresh ginger, season with salt and pepper, add ½ teaspoon of mustard oil and 3 tsps of lemon juice. Mix well either in a blender or with a pestle and mortar.

time by the cook, who ladles or spoons the rice and lentils and vegetables on to each plate, and second helpings are routinely offered. The meal is eaten noisily, with slurps and finger licking, and not-so-discreet belches at the end. All leftover food is offered to the animals in the house, the goats, chickens, dogs and buffalo. Meat is eaten on special occasions or festivals, perhaps twice a month, when a chicken or goat will be sacrificed.

For the first month of my stay I shared the trekkers' scorn for the incredibly well-balanced meal of *daal-bhaat-tarkari* (lentils, rice and vegetables), pining for chocolate and sugar and processed bread and biscuits. But as I got into the rural rhythms of walking and walking and yet more walking up hill and down dale, a subtle change in my neurochemistry emerged. The steaming bulk of a plate of staples to assuage hunger was a delight after walking nine hours to a distant health post.

Different shades of *daal* (yellow, pink, green and black) brought constant variety. Different seasonal vegetables introduced us to edible plants we had hardly ever seen (spiced spinach, squash blossoms, white radish, kohlrabi, fiddlehead ferns, black-eyed peas) and the selection of fresh chutneys and bottled pickles (*achaars*) based on ground marijuana (*gaaja*) seeds, tomatoes and onion, cucumber, bitter melon or spicy potato and sesame, brought a real tang and aftertaste to the meals. I learnt only one other culinary trick, not widely practiced in Nepal, when pickles were unavailable and there was a surfeit of rice: to squeeze fresh lemon or lime juice onto the steaming *bhaat*, which allowed one to eat vast quantities with a delicious citrus palate. For two years we lived a zero carbon existence, and ate a predominantly vegetarian, staple diet. We were never healthier nor happier.

Hot stuff!

I **Nick Hayes**
I UCL Division of Biosciences

Sex, war, pain, pleasure, castration and cookery! A melange of science and anecdote that will leave no bodice unripped, no swash unbuckled, no one undone!

Chillies: you eat them, they're hot, they can make you sweat, they can give you a burn – well obviously it's not a burn as they're not physically hot, but it certainly feels like one. So what's the story?

First let's think a bit about what chillies are. They're a fruit, they're generally succulent and highly coloured. What is the purpose of a fruit? A fruit is designed to be eaten, its colours are to attract the attention of its preferred diners. It is a capsule of seed with "Eat Me" written all over it. So why is it "hot"? It's hot because it wants to deter the wrong sort of diner. In fact, it wants to be eaten by a bird as the seed can withstand passage through a bird's gut, plus it gets distributed away from the parent plant, and also gets deposited with fertiliser. What it does not want to happen, is to be eaten by a mammal, as the seeds cannot withstand the more aggressive mammalian gut.

In order to put off the average mammal, chillies contain a chemical called capsaicin which gives chillies their "heat". Capsaicin interacts with a receptor that scientists call a Transient Receptor Potential Vanilloid 1 Receptor or TRPV1. TRPV1 is known as a "promiscuous receptor". This means that it responds to many stimuli, one of these being the protons that are released when skin is damaged by heat. It is messages from the nerves stimulated by TRPV1s that tell you, "Drop it! It's hot!" With milder forms of stimulation, and in concert with other receptors, TRPV1s may tell you that you are warm, or overheating. This is why you sweat when you eat a curry as a lot of your TRPV1s are telling the brain, "I'm being stimulated. You must be hot." The brain then takes what it thinks is appropriate action to cool you down.

Enough science.

SEX – Irritants have always been rubbed into the genitals by those souls mindful of the fact that irritants cause swelling. Don't try this at home!

WAR – The Aztecs lit fires of chillies upwind of the advancing Conquistadors, hoping that the wind would blow the pungent smoke into their eyes and blind them. In a slightly different sort of war, recalcitrant youths used to be hung upside down over a fire of dried chilli skins. Don't try this at home!

PAIN and PLEASURE – We've already talked about how chillies (or rather capsaicin) can stimulate nerves, and how this can sometimes be perceived as pain (for example: a chilli burn).

Interestingly this negative aspect of chillies fails to put people off eating them. There are a lot of theories as to why people eat chillies but they remain just that – theories. The most popular is that eating chillies releases endorphins (the body's equivalent of opiate drugs) giving a natural high.

I misquote from the *Tandoori Nights* TV series: "Who has not enjoyed the pleasure of a *jal frezi* in the evening, only to endure its exquisite pain the following morning?" Those of you who have done the above will have become only too aware of a part of the body blessed with apparently more than its fair share of TRPV1 receptors!

CASTRATION – Only eunuchs could work in the Chinese Imperial Court, so in order to apply for the job, one had to undergo surgery. The area to be operated on was rubbed with pepper-water (an infusion of black pepper, whose heat is still supplied by capsaicin, though in smaller quantities than chillies). We're not quite sure whether the idea was to desensitise the area to pain, or – like banging your head against a brick wall – whether the relief provided by losing the painful body parts outweighed the pain of the operation. Interestingly the last eunuch to be employed would apparently fly into a rage when confronted with a teapot. Don't try this at home!

Chilli popcorn:

Do try this at home!

Ingredients:

Popping corn
Oil
Chillies (the variety is up to you, people of a nervous disposition should avoid the Habanero/Scotch Bonnet or any of the Nagas)

To make:

Chop the chilli as fine as you want, and allow it to infuse in the oil, about a tablespoonful for a single layer of popping corn in a medium saucepan. Most of the heat occurs in the membranes and seeds of the chilli, which can be removed before infusion. Leave as long as you dare (overnight works). Strain and add to pan. Pour in popping corn, put over a medium to high heat and make sure you put the lid on. Shake occasionally. You will hear corn start to pop, when this slows down, remove from heat, wait a short time until popping has ceased and serve. You can play "Popcorn Roulette" by cooking a small amount of popcorn in an infusion of a hotter chillies and scattering these through either "unchillied" or mild chilli popcorn.

P.S.: Just in case you were wondering, birds don't have the TRPV1 receptor that responds to capsaicin.

Jam for social networking

I Dr. Rebecca Litchfield

In the age of Twitter, Facebook and smart-phones that can connect people to the world wide web at a moment's notice, it might seem strange to suggest that the age-old practice of preserving fruit and vegetables for use in other seasons can be used as a tool for social networking. Yet, it's remarkable what a world of local and global networks it can open up.

Two years ago I fell in with a crowd of Alaskan food bloggers and my life was changed forever. I want to share the development of my preserving obsession, the strange way in which it has opened up a whole new network of friends and a new-found understanding of the importance of these friendships, and the jams they have produced.

It all started with a much smaller food network: that between myself and my mother, who lives 300 miles away. I decided to start a blog as a way of literally showing my mum the things I was getting up to, mostly in the kitchen, and to recreate in cyberspace the feeling that we were sitting around the kitchen table together, because let's face it, blogging is the new "breaking bread" for the digital age.

As a result of this blog, I came across another one, started for almost the exact same reason; this blog was based in Alaska. One thing led to another and suddenly I was reading all about people like me who also loved food and loved sharing it with people. In October 2008, a second annual "jamming jelly exchange" was organised. Food bloggers from all over the world took part and swapped jars of jam with each other. "That sounds like fun", I thought to myself innocently. I threw my preserving pan into the mix and had a go. When a few weeks later, after wrapping, packing and nervously placing my jars in the care of the postal system of two countries, I spotted my humble jars of jam on someone else's blog in a kitchen thousands of miles away, it was such a thrill.

Jam crumble bars:

This recipe is a lovely and unusual way to use jam. It's infinitely adaptable, so you can use any flavour you like, add spices or citrus zest, or even, for a festive alternative, take it up a notch with a jar of mincemeat and a dash of brandy!

The following recipe makes approximately eight large slices, in a standard brownie pan of around 7" x 11". However it can easily be doubled for larger batches.

Ingredients:

Shortbread and crumble mix:
200g caster sugar
1 tsp baking powder
338g plain flour
250g cold unsalted butter
1 large egg
Zest of one lemon

For the jam filling:
350g jar of your favourite jam - blueberry and blackcurrant are great choices
Juice of one lemon
50ml water / or a spirit of your choice, such as brandy.

To make:

Preheat the oven to 190C. Grease and line your brownie pan.

In a medium bowl mix together the flour, sugar, zest and baking powder. Then, using your fingertips, a fork, or a pastry blender, mix in the egg and cold butter until the mixture resembles gravel.

Place 2/3 of this mixture into the prepared pan and press down to create and even layer that is compacted together. Place in the fridge to chill, and prepare your filling.

In a small saucepan, gently heat the jam, lemon juice and water/alcohol. Do not boil. When the mixture is nicely combined remove from the heat and allow to cool slightly.

Pour the jam mixture over the prepared base, gently smoothing to even across the whole surface. Then loosely scatter the remaining crumble mix over the top. You want to still be able to see glimpses of the jam filling below. Do not press down.

Place in the preheated oven and bake for 45 mins, or until the crumble topping is slightly golden. Remove onto a wire rack and cool completely before turning out and slicing.

Suddenly a whole new level of food knowledge and sharing was opened up. Our humble preserving of traditional produce and posting it to friends had made us all realise that the local or traditional produce we took for granted, was often completely alien to the person receiving the gift. I had no idea that my friend Nicole had never heard of green-gages, or tasted Seville marmalade. And I was perplexed when my return package arrived. A large jar of homemade salmonberry jam, a berry I'd never heard of. I also hadn't realised just how short Alaskan summers are, and so their need to preserve every precious berry and fruit was more than just a love of putting things in jars: it was a necessity.

Through the exchange of jams and the flurry of postcards, emails and blog posts that it produced, I had not only gained a whole new group of friends all the way across the world, but also a new level of respect for their needs and abilities. These people did it for the love, but also because they wanted the summer produce in December, when the sun barely makes it above the horizon. No wonder they were obsessed with jam and all its magic properties!

In the last two years, my obsession with all forms of preserving has taken me on an amazing food and friendship journey. I have sent my preserves across the world and seen them on other people's blogs, sitting in kitchens in Alaska. I have filled a friend's wedding cake with my favourite homemade jam, provided it for brunches and sold it in markets to people from all over the place. Making jam has provided me with a way of social networking in a way I never thought possible.

Jam has made me even more aware of the seasonality of food, and the great variation of food across the world. I've managed to try fruits I'd never even heard of before. Most of all though, making jam and being passionate about homemade food has connected me with a whole host of new people and places. People and places I would never have had contact with otherwise. Two years ago, I didn't even own a preserving pan, now, with help from people all over the place, I have my own business and am networking with shop owners in my community who are excited to be selling a local, seasonal, homemade product. I preserve, and that's all the social networking I need!

Kilburn station planters

I **Sanchia Dunn**
I Transition Town

Our local Transition Town[1] food group was regularly looking for new spaces to grow food in the area. "What about the neglected planters at Kilburn tube station?" came the idea.

It seemed rather ambitious, but also quite obvious, given that this station on the London Underground network is a well-used and high profile transport hub in this part of London (with almost 12,000 journeys in and out everyday). It would be the perfect place to inspire fellow residents and commuters, and share information about the Transition network and local food issues.

The response to our initial contact with London Underground was expectedly bureaucratic: "We've checked with management and those beds are for flowers not for growing food." A little deflated, it took a whole year and the creation of a few other allotment sites in the rest of our area before we tried again. This time we had resigned ourselves to the fact that we would only be allowed ornamental plants, but were steeled by a slightly furtive plan to include as many edible ornamentals as we could.

[1] Transition towns are local, community-led initiatives that work to make communities more resilient to the challenges of peak oil and climate change. See www. transitionnetwork.org for more information.

We included plenty of herbs, and a few plants with edible fruits and flowers were also on the list. We had a plan that we thought would win them over – plants that were attractive, low maintenance, drought resistant and attractive to wildlife.

We soon scheduled a meeting with London Underground and were ready to talk them through our illustrated presentation leaflet, which included a secret arsenal of edibles. We met with a Group Station Manager who, as soon as we'd been introduced, sat down and pushed some papers across the table in our direction. "Underground in Bloom 2011" read the first page, and was followed by sheets of competition information and judging categories. It seems that this time we'd approached them at just the right time to coincide with an internal London Underground competition to see which station could grow the best gardens, with options to enter different categories. Our eyes scanned the list of categories stopping at one claiming to be new this year: "Grow your own", for fruit and vegetable gardens. We decided to avoid discussion of the ornamental planting plan.

There seems to be an instinctive paranoia that we all have towards living things in urban contexts. Cities are the concrete, built-up products of human ideas. They're about design, control and manageable risk. Plants don't fit very well into this plan. That is, unless they're: a) predictable, overused,

"amenity" plants; b) plastic; or c) being removed with herbicide or a chainsaw. Add to this health and safety-related concerns about pollution absorbed by food grown in a city and on a train platform, and people easily become negative about food growing projects. Cities do have higher concentrations of pollution than the surrounding countryside, but does that make it a good reason not to try and grow at least something?

At our meeting the discussion had now moved so far away from what we'd originally been expecting. The station manager still wanted an impressive floral display, but we were now also talking about what sorts of fruits and vegetables we should plant. We tried not to look too elated, but inside my co-volunteer and I we were both jumping around like excited kids. We were going to plant an actual allotment on a tube station platform!

Eventually, we organised a planting day for the end of May 2011. London Underground had been given a small competition budget for each station entering. We had some incredibly positive involvement from a local garden centre (Hampstead Garden Centre), who donated a large amount of plants and materials on top of what was purchased within the budget. It took a little co-ordination to ensure our work on the platform planters created minimal disturbance to passengers, but eventually we had ten volunteers on the platform carrying equipment back and forth, digging in

Commuters' herb salad:

This salad is ideal for our commuters' allotment. You don't need too much of any one ingredient, and substitutions are easy. We've planted most of these plants below in the station planters.

Ingredients:

Mixed salad leaves - torn into pieces. Include any spinach or chard leaves too
Parsley - chopped or snipped coarsely
Marjoram - leaves trimmed off stems
Basil - leaves, trimmed off stems
Chive tops - snipped into inch long pieces
Mint leaves - trimmed off stems, and torn into smaller pieces

Other good allotment products include: cherry tomatoes, radishes, turnip tops, baby carrots. Cut these into bite sized pieces and add to the leaves. Because of all the strong, fresh flavours this salad rarely needs much dressing, but add to taste.

To make:

Mix well and serve with almost anything!

Great with cheese sandwiches (or inside them).

compost, planting flowers, herbs, fruit and vegetables, and carting watering cans back and forth.

The plants are now in and have begun to receive some positive responses from passengers. We're watching to see how they grow and whether people take us up on our invitation to "help yourself, but leave enough for others". And if they do, we'll be watching their faces as they take a bite into that strawberry.

Making universities into better neighbours

I **Dr. Hilary Jackson and Dr. Gemma Moore**
I UCL Public Engagement Unit

Public engagement has emerged as a major force in higher education. However, the term can mean many things to many people. Different definitions shift the emphasis in subtle but important ways; even the best definitions can make you think 'yes, but what actually happens?'.

It can feel like public engagement means throwing lots of ingredients together (ideas, methods of engagement, people) and hoping for an edible outcome. Using our experience of supporting over 70 projects as part of UCL's Public Engagement Unit, we present a recipe for successful public engagement.

The activities we support vary widely. For example, we've funded meetings of patients, researchers and healthcare professionals working together to guide medical research. We've also worked with academics supporting community interest groups so that their voices are heard by the city government. Of course, one of the most successful activities has been the wonderful *Food Junctions*, which brought UCL staff and students from more than twenty different de-partments together with citizens from outside the university, sharing expertise from inside and outside to create thought-provoking, practical and fascinating events focused on the subject of food.

Maybe because of the incredible variety of public engagement activities that the Public Engagement Unit at UCL has been involved in, we've found that every activity contains a unique blend of ingredients. However, we think that there are some ingredients that no successful public engagement activity can go without.

Firstly, public engagement activities must be developed from the needs of all parties involved. Universities can

only operate with the support of society. This isn't just because they are funded by tax-payers, it's also because they are dependent on a culture that permits free thought and is open to challenges. University staff and students also benefit from a different perspective on their work, as well as guidance on what they do.

Moreover, there's no point in university staff and students creating public activities that meet no public need. The most successful activities begin with the need of a group of people outside the university. This might be a need for support, for information, for expertise, or a need to be heard, understood, or represented in society. University staff and students seeking to meet a public need must think about how they can best help, working together with the people they are seeking to engage with to ensure that the activities are interesting, relevant and timed to suit all concerned.

Recognising needs on both sides, and working together on public engagement projects, generates mutual respect that continues long beyond the end of an activity. Transparency is key to this: hidden goals on either side can negate this mutual respect.

If successful public engagement begins with an acknowledgement of needs, that means it should have an impact on all participants – whether they are citizens outside the university or within. The only way to ensure this is to set out with

clear aims and objectives, as well as a good idea of what success looks like. In order to make sure you're not creeping away from your aims, and to know what you've achieved, build in time for reflection, evaluation and learning throughout the project.

The final, crucial ingredients are the skills and energy of everyone involved. The people are the most important part of public engagement. Expertise and resources brought by all participants must be valued in order for enthusiasm to be maintained.

Successful public engagement activities can't be created by throwing lots of ingredients together and hoping for the best. We feel that by using the ingredients we've described, a delicious outcome is certain.

www.ucl.ac.uk/public-engagement
publicengagement@ucl.ac.uk

Mapping local food for change

| Chris Church

| Mapping for Change

The expansion of projects within the field of 'local food' has been a key feature of activity around sustainability during the past decade

In London this work has been boosted by initiatives such as 'Capital Growth', seeking to develop 2012 new local food projects by the time of the Olympics, while the Big Lottery Fund's 'Local Food' programme has also funded much good and innovative work.

Food is perhaps the most obvious consumer focus for local sustainability work, so it is important that consumers know what is happening where, and what is available. Equally those developing projects need to have a clear picture of who is doing what. But with so much happening, one simple listing will never be enough. That's one reason why local food mapping has taken off alongside food growing.

The first project to work on this was Big Barn, set up in 2002 and still going strong. Big Barn (www.bigbarn.co.uk/aboutus/) serves consumers and is a Community Interest Company set up as an on-line market to "help people to find good, safe, accountable food from local sources". Big Barn's early use of on-line mapping helped the London 21 Sustainability Network to develop the world's first on-line 'green map' of a city. From that work, London 21 developed other mapping projects and in doing so made links with academics working on participatory mapping at University College London.

From this cooperation emerged a new social enterprise, Mapping for Change (MfC – www.mappingforchange.org.uk). MfC is jointly owned by University College London and London 21 and works to "promote and support community-based initiatives towards building more sustainable communities through the use of maps and geographic information". MfC has advised various local mapping processes on food and sustainability issues, and has incorporated mapping of local food projects into work such as the UK map of local climate change action (www.communitymaps.org.uk/ukclimateaction). It also has links with other food maps such as Somerset's 'FoodMapper' (www.foodmapper.org.uk)

MfC specialises in participatory mapping, working with projects and communities. This is particularly relevant to local food since there are so many small and very local projects and the knowledge of who is doing what is very dispersed. This approach is also important to develop new areas of work as food mapping goes beyond simply mapping growers and retailers. FoodMapper now helps people find land potentially available for community growing and links groups looking for land.

In London there's a new focus at the other end of the 'food chain' – food waste. Food waste is a critical issue – it's estimated that up to one third of the food produced across the world goes to waste. It's a particular problem in London, with a very dense and mobile population and tens of thousands of food retailers from supermarkets to corner stores and cafés. Most throw away food every day which is perfectly safe to eat, while at the same time there are many people in London so poor that they cannot afford to buy enough food for themselves and their families. MfC is now working with 'Plan Zheroes' a new project from the London Citizens' 'Greener Planet Action Team' to tackle this issue (www.planzheroes.org/get-involved).

Mapping can play a key part in help-ing food which would otherwise go to landfill get to the people who really need it. It poses some specific problems: food doesn't stay safe for long, so up-to-date information is important. A map also has to work for large and small retail-ers and for the wide variety of charities, day centres, etc. that support poor and homeless people. It will also need to be open to those who have 'one-off' sup-plies of surplus food, such as festival caterers, conferences and so forth. One feature of MfC's mapping is that regis-tered map users can sign up to get texts to their phones when new events are posted on a map – this may help ensure rapid uptake of food on offer.

Local food action is innovating and flourishing all over London and the UK. Mapping is one way in which informa-tion about all this work can be made easily accessible. Mapping for Change is looking to make sure that happens.

Matters of taste

| Sanna Hirvonen

| Department of Philosophy, UCL

When people say "It's just a matter of taste", what they mean is that there is no unique, right answer to the issue under discussion. How foods or drinks taste to people are taken to be a paradigm example of a 'matter of taste': *De gustibus non est disputandum*, as the Ancient Romans once said.

But if that's the case then why do we actively engage in disputes about taste? It's perfectly commonplace to have discussions or disagreements over whether some dish, drink or ingredient tastes good or bad, delicious, tasty, disgusting and so on. To see the problem, first imagine two people who are tasting a novel dish and they try to distinguish the ingredients used in making it. There is clearly an answer to the question, and each time they disagree ("It has carrot" - "No, that's pumpkin"), only one of them can get it right. But now, imagine that one of them says the dish is delicious and the other disagrees. Is only one of them right?

Many people would side with the Ancient Romans and answer "no": one of them likes the dish, the other doesn't, and that's the end of the story. But what if one of the tasters is an expert in cooking? We start to feel that maybe they know better given their experience. Whether something tastes pleasant or unpleasant involves learning: we've all gone through the experience of coming to like an item we used to find disgusting. So maybe the taste of food isn't just a question of personal preferences but of knowledge and experience which is why some people have good taste regarding food. Few people would think that a person who only eats frozen pizzas and a master chef have an equally good taste. Maybe the person who only eats pizza simply isn't competent enough to make claims about the quality of foods due to her limited experience.

So should we conclude that in the end, we can have reasonable disagreements over taste and the one who has a better taste is the one who gets it right? Empirical evidence suggests that the picture is more complicated than that. For example, people can be divided into non-tasters, tasters, and supertasters regarding how a chemical 6-n-propylthiouracil (PROP) tastes to them. As the name indicates, non-tasters don't taste the chemical whereas to the supertaster it tastes unpleasantly bitter. The natural relative of the chemical is present in a variety of vegetables and other foodstuffs, causing them to taste bitter to the supertaster. The difference is genetic rather than acquired, and the three groups are thought to be roughly equally large with some differences in distribution between genders and around the globe.

Now, imagine that a non-taster, taster and a supertaster are judging say, a bowl of broccoli soup. If the non-taster thinks it's delicious, the taster that it's OK and the supertaster that it's nasty and bitter, ought we say that only one of them is right? If so, which one? Given that there's roughly an equal amount of each kind of taster in the world it doesn't seem that any of them is the abnormal one. Perhaps we should conclude that each of them is right relative to the group of tasters they represent. That seems right since it doesn't prejudge one way of tasting over another. But now, let us return to our earlier question about taste and experience. Isn't it possible to learn to like bitter tastes? Most coffee drinkers find it bitter at first but then grow to like it. So it's not clear that a supertaster couldn't grow to like the bitterness she tastes in so many foods.

Currently there simply isn't an answer to the question of how much experience can affect one's taste preferences, and what is the extent of our genetic differences. What we do know is the variability among us, which is enough to discourage the idea that if we disagree about taste one of us must be getting it wrong. So, even a picky eater can be right when she judges most foods disgusting. However, since experience matters, the picky eater can train herself to like more things even if it's not fun at first. Liking more things makes it much easier to get pleasure from food so the effort is worth it.

That brings us to my final point. Since our tastes are adaptable, why not intentionally adapt them towards the healthy, easy to cook and ecological? If there is any point to the idea of a good or bad taste, it should rather be found in a taste that's good for the eater as well as her environment. We are not determined by nature to remain what we are at birth, be it regarding our abilities, taste, knowledge or preferences. What we eat is one of the important choices we make, and thanks to our adaptability we can learn to like food that keeps us healthy and saves other creatures as well as our environment. In the end, liking may be a matter of taste, but we are free to influence which kind of taste we come to have.

Milk drinking and evolution

| Professor Mark G. Thomas

| Research Department of Genetics, Evolution and Environment UCL

Most Europeans take drinking milk for granted; it's the everyday consumption of an everyday drink. But for most adult humans, indeed, for most adult mammals, milk is very far from an everyday drink.

Milk is something that we have only recently evolved to be able to consume, and Darwin's engine of evolutionary change, natural selection, has probably worked harder on this ability than on any other biological characteristic of Europeans in the last 10,000 years.

It has been known at least since Roman times that individuals vary in their ability to digest milk. The reason for this is that as adults, most people in the world stop producing the enzyme lactase shortly after weaning. This enzyme is produced in the small intestine and is essential to digest the main sugar in milk: lactose. When lactase is absent, gut bacteria get an extra treat, and this is where the problems like diarrhoea and chronic flatulence[1] start. Such people are described as lactase non-persistent, or lactose intolerant.

Lactase persistent people produce lactase throughout adulthood. This is a genetic trait with a very uneven global

distribution (Figure 1); it is particularly common in Europe and some African, Middle Eastern and southern Asian peoples, but relatively rare elsewhere. However, in recent years scientists have discovered that there are multiple genetic causes, which means that it must have evolved independently a number of times.

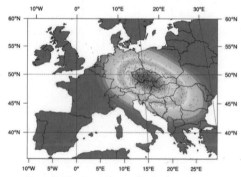

Figure 1: The approximate distribution of lactase persistence in the Old World.

Using genetic data from living people it is possible to get an idea of how old these various lactase gene variants are. They seem to have originated in the last 10,000 or so years – very recently on the human evolution time-scale. Furthermore, if we see a gene variant that is common but young then it is possible to estimate how strong the force of natural selection was in favouring that variant[2]. The idea here is that while it is possible for an unselected variant to change its frequency slowly over time – simply by chance – it takes an extra kick (i.e. a selective advantage) to drive a rapid increase in frequency. Using this approach the lactase gene really does stand out; a 'Mount Everest' of natural selection when compared to the rest of the genome.

It is difficult to envisage large numbers of adults consuming fresh milk in the past without the presence of domestic animals. Because of this, the evolution of lactase persistence and the development of dairying are thought to have gone hand-in-hand; we call this a gene-culture co-evolutionary process. But what became common first, dairying or lactase persistence? The growing field of bioarchaeology has something to say here. Firstly, Joachim Burger and colleagues extracted DNA from the bones of some early European farmers[3], and managed to show that lactase persistence was considerably less common than it is today.

Secondly, Richard Evershed and colleagues were able to identify dairy fats on pots made by the earliest European farmers[4], indicating that milk was being produced before people could comfortably consume it. This isn't as strange as it sounds. Milk can be processed to make yoghurt, butterfat and cheese by fermentation, a process that reduces or almost entirely removes lactose while still preserving many of the other nutrients.

So what was the big advantage that drinking fresh milk gave our ancestors? Although we don't know the correct answer, there are plenty of suggestions including:

1. being a protein, fat and energy rich food;
2. being a relatively uncontaminated fluid, other water sources were likely to contain parasites;
3. the regularity of supply of nutrients, as opposed to the 'boom-and-bust' of seasonal crops;
4. the possibility that early dairy farming was more economical than crop-only farming; and
5. the value of milk as a supply of vitamin D and calcium in northern latitudes[5].

Another big question is where and when did lactase persistence first evolve in Europe? When geneticists want to work out where a particular gene variant originated they usually look for where it is most common. In Europe, lactase persistence is most common in north-west Europe, especially Scandinavia and Ireland. But we already know that the earliest European dairying populations were located in southeast Europe. If the genetics of lactase persistence co-evolved with the culture of dairying

[1] Swallow, D. M. (2003). Genetics of lactase persistence and lactose intolerance. *Annual Review of Genetics.* 37: 197-219

[2] Bersaglieri, T., et al. (2004). Genetic signatures of strong recent positive selection at the lactase gene. *American Journal of Human Genetics.* 74(6): 1111-1120

[3] Burger, J., et al. (2007). Absence of the lactase-persistence-associated allele in early Neolithic Europeans. *Proceedings of the National Academy of Sciences.* 104(10): 3736.

[4] Evershed, R. P., et al. (2008). Earliest date for milk use in the Near East and southeastern Europe linked to cattle herding. *Nature.* 455: 528–531.

[5] Flatz, G. and Rotthauwe, H. W. (1973). Lactose nutrition and natural selection. *The Lancet.* 302(7820): 76–77.

then how do we make sense of these two seemingly contradictory facts?

The best solution to this problem is to simulate our evolutionary past in a computer; that is, to model how lactase persistence and dairying spread. Using this approach lactase persistence was found to have first provided an evolutionary advantage about 7,500 years ago in a region covering the modern-day Czech Republic, Slovakia, Austria and Hungary (Figure 2). What happens in the process of spread is that the genetic variant causing lactase persistence gets carried forward towards northwest Europe on a wave of advancing farmers, much like a surfer rides a wave at sea.

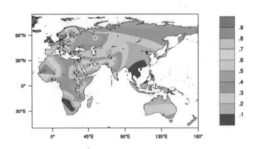

Figure 2: The inferred location where lactase persistence first underwent natural selection among dairy farmers.

What is particularly exciting about this origin time and location is that it is when and where the first major farming culture of northern Europe, the Linearbandkeramik (Linear Pottery culture), started to spread from its homeland – in modern-day Hungary – to cover much of northern Europe. What is more, archaeological research tells us that at

Figure 3: Linearbandkeramik pottery. Was this the pottery of the world's first fresh milk drinking adults?

this time, the Linearbandkeramik people reduced their reliance on goats and sheep and increased their use of cattle. The Linearbandkeramik people are best known for their pottery style – rounded with painted lines or 'bands' (Figure 3) – and their apparently rapid movement from their homeland to northwestern Europe in less than 400 years. Could it be that these pots were designed primarily to carry milk? Were the Linearbandkeramik people so mobile because cows are easier to move than growing crops? So far this scenario fits well with archaeological and both ancient and modern DNA data.

The story of the evolution of milk drinking and dairying is still far from complete. We still don't know why it was such a big evolutionary advantage and many details of the archaeology and genetics need to be filled in. One thing is certain though: it will require interdisciplinary research between geneticists, archaeologists, anthropologists, nutritionists and computer modellers to fully understand this, the most important dietary adaptation in humans in the last 10,000 years.

Milkshake exclusif

| Sam Bompas
| Jellymongers

McDonald's meals are almost perfect in terms of giving your body what it craves. The carefully calibrated combination of fat, salt and sugar makes the food compelling.

It stimulates neurons, cells that trigger the brain's reward system and release dopamine, a chemical that motivates our behavior and makes us want to eat more. Many of us have what's called a "bliss point", at which we get the greatest pleasure from sugar, fat or salt. Combined in the right way, they make a product indulgent and high in "hedonic value".

McDonald's gets this pretty much spot on. In terms of "hedonic value" you can't get more for your money.

Only two things are missing from the ultimate 'happy meal'. Proper table-cloths and alcohol. If you combine these elements with your usual burger meal it'll be unforgettable. It's not too hard to do with a bit of forward planning. We like to take white tablecloths, napkins and silver candelabra when we visit McDonald's. You get some strange looks but it's worth it in terms of the *frisson* of danger. We also like to take a bottle of Courvoisier Exclusif to add to our milkshakes. This is hugely rewarding for the level of depth and complexity it adds to the shake.

Milkshake exclusif:

Ingredients:
1 medium vanilla milkshake
1 heavy slug of Courvoisier Exclusif

To make:
Drink the milkshake down enough to slip in a heavy slug of Courvoisier Exclusif when the McDonald's branch manager isn't looking.
Give it a stir with your red, yellow and white straw and enjoy.
As a bonus grate some fresh black truffles on your nuggets.

More than stuffed dormice

I Dr. Debbie Challis

I UCL Petrie Museum of Egyptian Archaeology

One of the best known descriptions of a Roman banquet comes from *The Satyricon* by Gaius Petronius (c.27-66 CE), a Roman courtier in the reign of Nero. 'Trimalchio's dinner' in *The Satyricon* is a satirical account of a dinner party.

The banquet's obscenely rich food is used as a distorted mirror to reflect the greed and pretensions of the vulgar host Trimalchio. It was this banquet that chef Heston Blumenthal re-created in his series on historic cookery for Channel 4 in 2009[1]. Very few Romans, if any, ate like that. The average fare was barley, cabbage, cooked meat (if lucky!) and cheese.

Recipes resembling food described in *The Satyricon*, including stuffed dormice, are in the recipe texts known as 'Apicius', the sole survivor of a collection of recipes from the first century CE put together about 400 years later. This collection of recipes was named after Marcus Gavius Apicius, a notorious gourmand during the reign of Tiberius (14-37 CE). The collection was put together by various cooks from wealthy Roman homes, who were probably slaves or freedmen. The *Apicius* is a collection of recipes cooked for those at the top of the social classes by those at the bottom. However, it does include some 'everyday' food.

[1] For more on the banquet see Mary Beard, 'Heston's Roman feast', A Don's Life. Weblog. (http://tinyurl.com/crf58e), (accessed 28 April 2011).

Archaeological evidence gives us a wider perspective on what was eaten. The Petrie Museum of Egyptian Archaeology at UCL has cooking pots, kitchen equipment and dried food. There are also the remains of kitchens and taverns in Pompeii and other Roman sites. We know that some Roman troops on Hadrian's Wall ate food from a kind of North African terrine because archaeologists have excavated the pots. We also know that these troops ate food from across the Empire – such as hops from the Netherlands – due to traces in living areas and in latrines.

Roman food had been heavily influenced by Greek traditions of cooking, but was adapted to Roman tastes. What the Romans ate evolved over centuries and was informed by the Empire. Roman cuisine was a hotchpotch of different tastes and influences based on access to food commodities. The names of dishes reflected places in the Empire, such as 'pyramid cakes' made out of heaped oats and honey. The Romans did not have many of the ingredients we take for granted today, such as sugar, tomatoes and potatoes and their combination of flavours was quite different.

Fish sauce, or *garum*, was important in flavouring Roman food. Historians disagree about its use and variety, but Thai fish sauce is thought to be similar. Other 'strange' flavour combinations include honey and peppercorns. For example, boiling dates in honey, pepper and a glass of wine works well. Honey

Alexandrine bread dip:

This is a recipe based on No. 127 in Book IV of the *Apicius (Salacaccabia*: literally 'salted food boiled in a pot').

To make:

Hollow out an Alexandrine loaf of bread (crusty bread with cumin added; you can add the cumin later into the bread crumb mix if not making the bread from scratch), soak the crumbs with a mixture of water, wine vinegar or lemon juice and make a paste of it. Combine pepper, 1 tbsp honey, big bunch of mint, 3 cloves crushed garlic, big bunch of coriander, salted cheese (parmesan), water and oil in a mortar. Then add this mixture to the bread crumbs and pour 1-2 tbsps of wine over.

Put the mixture back into the crusty loaf and serve with celery sticks.

and fruit were used in lots of savoury dishes, such as leeks with apple and honey. Cumin and a variety of different herbs were used and combined in marinades and sauces. Other features, such as cooking in wine, are similar to contemporary cooking.

The *Apicius* does not record cooking techniques, though archaeological evidence gives us clues. The two-handled cooking pot pictured is a stewing pot, or *pultarius*. One of the few techniques named in the *Apicius* is grinding ingredients, and so mortars were essential to Roman kitchens. Only high status homes had a dining room and a kitchen, most Romans ate out. There were also no *vomitoria*, vomiting was usually connected with drunkenness.

And so, there is more to Roman food than stuffed dormice. In fact their legacy is still with us since Roman cuisine, with its use of olive oil, mixing flavours, and lots of pepper and garlic, laid the foundations of modern Mediterranean cooking.

For more cooking ideas see:

Sally Grainger, *Cooking Apicius: Roman Recipes for Today.* London: Prospect Books; 2006.

Mark Grant, Roman Cookery: *Ancient Recipes for Modern Kitchens.* London: Serif; 2008.

Jane Renfrew, *Roman Cookery: Recipes and History.* English Heritage; 2004.

Mulberry ice

I **Andy Hulme**

The mulberry has perhaps the most intense flavour of any fruit, a supercharged raspberry with a rich, almost woody taste, but its extreme fragility and perishability make it an extremely unusual commercial product.

I saw an old recipe which began "Should you be fortunate enough to have a Mulberry Tree in your garden" but in a sense we all have as it's not an uncommon tree, often found in rather delightful public places. Its six week succession of abundant ripe fruits makes it

an ideal source of luxury urban forage. The written Chinese word for mulberry (*sang shen*) means "tree picked by many hands". If you can find a good one at the right time, there will be fruit to pick, unless you have the misfortune to follow a citizen greedy for the hallucinogenic properties of the young green fruits. As well as vitamins and assorted 'wonder drugs', the mulberry is a rich source of myth and legend, up there with the oak and the apple. Here's one:

One sunny afternoon four and a half thousand years ago Leizu, wife of the Yellow Emperor, was enjoying a cup of tea in the shade of a mulberry tree when a small object dropped from above into her cup. It was a cocoon. On removing it, she found that, softened by the hot tea, a single filament a mile long and not easily broken unravelled from it.

Silk. The resourceful Empress planted groves of mulberry trees, learned how to farm the caterpillars and invented the reel and the loom. Meanwhile husband Huang Di, in legend at least, was taming animals, domesticating crops, codifying medicine and founding Chinese civilisation.

Mulberry ice:

To make:

1. Pick 2-3 cups of the fruit.
2. Wash.
3. Make syrup with 1 cup sugar, 1 cup water, a few drops of lemon juice. Boil for 2 minutes. Allow to partially cool.
4. Add mulberries to warm syrup. Leave for five minutes.
5. The seeds of the mulberry are soft so the fruit can just be mashed into the syrup as it cools.
6. When the mixture has cooled right down, mix in one cup of Greek yoghurt.
7. Put the container you intend to use in the freezer a couple of hours beforehand.
8. A heavy cast iron pan pre-frozen is almost as good as an ice cream machine, but anything will do.
9. Put mixture in container and place in the freezer. Take out and stir every 30 minutes. Should be ready in 2 hours.

The White Mulberry tree, which is native to China, has rather poor fruit, but is the best for feeding the silk moth caterpillars. The Black Mulberry originated in south-western Asia and by classical times was cultivated in Greece. The Romans later brought it to England. Ovid wrote down the story of Pyramus and Thisbe, whose assignation under a mulberry tree goes badly wrong. Thisbe arrives first, is frightened away by a lion, its mouth bloody from a fresh kill. Unfortunately she drops her scarf which the lion playfully mauls. Confronted with this scene, Pyramus surmises that Thisbe has been devoured and promptly stabs himself to death whereupon she returns and borrows his sword to kill herself. Spurting blood stains some of the hitherto white fruits. The gods decide to change the colour of all the fruit in honour of the lovers, a real messy metamorphosis, but with a certain poetic essence. The fruits do ripen through bright red to a blackish dried blood colour.

Shakespeare lampooned it in *A Midsummer Nights Dream* where Bottom and company present a farcical performance of the story. In retirement at New Place in Stratford he planted a mulberry in his garden. In 1752 a subsequent owner of the property, Reverend Francis Gastrell, irritated by the attentions of sightseers, demolished the house and cut down the tree. Numerous busts, cups and snuffboxes were made from the wood, and cuttings from the tree propagated, to make the claim of being "Shakespeare's Mulberry". There's one in the garden of Garrick's House at Hampton and a cutting from that has made the return journey to Stratford.

It was in Shakespeare's time that the silk industry finally arrived in England having taken millennia to spread from central China, although trade in the cloth had been going for two or three centuries. King James I set about planting 10,000 trees, many in London, at Greenwich and on four acres which are now part of the gardens of Buckingham Palace. It may have been one of them that Shakespeare acquired. The silk farming venture was not a success. The leaves of the Black Mulberries that the King had used may not have been to the caterpillars' taste. He eventually moved the operation to Virginia where they happily gorged themselves on the American Red Mulberry. The proliferation of mulberries in London is attributed to James's efforts, but it is doubtful if any of the venerable looking trees that survive today are quite that old. They tend to be found in parks and gardens laid out in the early 19th century, like the three very fine ones in West Square, Lambeth. It is the habit of the Black Mulberry to spread its branches very widely then to fall over at the earliest opportunity and continue growing quite happily in a prostrate condition. This can make them look very old indeed.

It would be nice to think that a few of the Jacobean trees survived changes in land use to be incorporated into later schemes but the odds are always against this. In February 2011 readers of the *Daily Mail* were informed:

They stain the pavements: Council's bizarre excuse for chopping down mulberry trees at historic London park.

Anybody who cares to search "Vauxhall mulberry trees" will find this saga of urban regeneration extremely well documented. The old trees were destroyed and replaced by two new "mature" nursery grown mulberries planted a few yards away. The trees are dead. Long live the trees!

Mulligatawny soup and "authentic" curry

| Divya Narayanan
| University of Virginia

Many around the world today are familiar with Indian food, or at least, with some variation of it. Of course, cuisines and food cultures on the Indian subcontinent are characterised by a great diversity of culinary traditions.

People both in and outside India are likely to think of the subcontinent's gastronomic repertoire as being characterized by rich, aromatic and spicy flavours. Dishes such as *dal*, curry, *biryani*, *korma* and *dopiaza* have become popular in many parts of the world. In Britain, especially, Indian food has become popular enough to have been indigenised to a great extent.

One would imagine that all these world-conquering Indian dishes must be of considerable antiquity, likely perfected at the tables of Mughal emperors, as many an Indian restaurant menu would have us believe. The truth is rather more complicated for the Indian subcontinent's culinary repertoire is built up of layers of interlocking traditions, and has accepted and internalised much in the last few centuries.

Historians of food and agriculture will tell you that vegetables we consider intrinsic to Indian food – such as chillies, potatoes, and tomatoes – are in fact not indigenous. These foods from the New World did not begin to make an entry into everyday Indian cooking until sometime during the eighteenth century. Indians never actually called their sauce based dishes 'curry' until the British popularized the term. So, our common Indian curry of today, based on an onion and tomato sauce and generously seasoned with chillies, is something of very recent origin.

There is a unique manuscript[1] that provides an interesting illustration of the dynamic manner in which culinary

[1] Untitled MS from the British Library (Untitled MS BM OR 2028).

Nan Khatai:
Makes around 40 biscuits

Ingredients:

150g all-purpose flour
100g semolina
100g castor sugar
100g butter
½ tsp green cardamom powder
¼ tsp nutmeg powder
¼ tsp saffron
¼ tsp cinnamon powder
½ tsp baking soda
1 tsp milk
1 tsp thick yoghurt
Crushed pistachios to garnish

To make:

Sieve the all-purpose flour and semolina 2 to 3 times. To this flour mixture, add the cardamom, nutmeg, cinnamon, saffron, baking soda, milk and yoghurt. Mix well.

Whisk the butter and sugar together into a smooth paste. Now, slowly add the flour mix to the batter, while constantly mixing and folding. Knead well till smooth and pliable. Allow the dough to stand for around thirty minutes at room temperature, then shape into small balls. Grease a baking tray and lightly dust with flour.

Arrange the balls on this tray with a 3-4 inch gap between them. Gently tap the top and carve a small cross to allow the escape of heat. Sprinkle the crushed pistachios and pat lightly to embed them in the dough.

Bake in an oven at 150 degrees Celsius for around thirty minutes. The biscuits should be lightly browned. Allow to cool before removing the biscuits from the baking tray. Enjoy!

cultures interact. It is a Persian translation of an English cookbook, dating from 1801. It details some typical European dishes: recipes for tomato soup, vegetable soup, mock turtle soup and hare soup; entrées such as beef fillet, various kinds of stew, steak and mutton chop, mashed potatoes, and macaroni; as well as desserts such as apple dumplings, tartlets, and Shrewsbury cake. But it also has multiple recipes for mulligatawny soup, and makes reference to 'curry' and 'curry powder'. The interesting thing is that such recipes never existed in any Indo-Persian cookbook at the time. Indians who read this cookbook must have thought these to be exotic European dishes.

Yet these dishes did have an Indian ancestry. Even though there are many competing theories for the origin of the term 'curry', various curry recipes undoubtedly draw on Asian culinary influences. Mulligatawny soup has an interesting story. The name 'mulligatawny' most likely derived from the Tamil phrase *mulaga tanni*, literally meaning 'pepper water', and its recipe is of South Indian origin. Elements of this dish must have travelled from South Indian kitchens to Europe along with travellers, traders, and missionaries. Then its highly anglicised variation seems to have found its way back into the Indian subcontinent through this translated cookbook, and may even have been cooked in a North Indian kitchen!

'Indian food' as we know it today is as diverse as the people on this vast subcontinent. Many peoples have travelled through, or migrated to India over the past several centuries: Central Asians, Iranians, Arabs, Armenians, Abyssinians, Chinese, Portuguese, Dutch, and English, to name a few. Indian food cultures have thus influenced, and been influenced by, various culinary traditions.

Now, here is a question to consider, a 'recipe' for thought. When we talk about 'authentic' Indian food, what do we really mean? After all, what we consider 'authentic' today was once foreign. Culinary traditions are in a constant state of creation. Food recipes, as we have seen, are circulated and re-circulated dynamically through different cultural realms. 'Indian cuisine' was and is created at the junctions of various food cultures. That is what makes it so delectable.

New dishes on the table

I Clayton Chiang

I Green Hope Project of Asia-Pacific

There is no better time for us to choose and practice a new diet than now.

Our primary aim must be to prevent an ecological calamity occurring on earth by stopping our consumption of meat and radically changing our diet. If we are not bold enough to do this, the earth as we know it will be doomed. Fortunately, it appears that a positive food revolution is on the rise.

A range of research institutions have assessed the extent of our ecological crisis with a wide range of results. The main reason for this lack of agreement is that most researchers use a reductionist framework in their analysis, rather than considering the earth in a ecological and holistic way. To combine independent factors would make a study impossibly complex and time-consuming.

As early as 2006, the United Nations had already informed countries around the world that they should change their national food policies and stop supporting livestock breeding as a means of saving the earth from ecological catastrophe. However, most political leaders are only concerned with their votes and the views of food industry stakeholders who will perceive any new policies as too drastic and not in their interest. It is hard to imagine that any political leader will have the wisdom and commitment to actively lead the much-needed revolution in the food production and catering industries.

If the revolution is difficult to carry out from top down, the question is - might it be possible to generate one from the bottom up? There are a range of reasons for people not coming together to solve the problem.

First of all, most people do not have sufficient knowledge of vegetarianism. The meat and dairy industries with their vested interests and huge profits are reluctant to change their business model. People do not make all-out attempts to promote plant-based diets. Vegetarians mainly communicate with fellow vegetarians, which cannot reach, let alone touch the heart of, the general public. The negative impact of meat eating on the human body, mind and spirit, and the degree of hazard posed to global ecology, have not been known by the general public until very recently. Secondly, there is a blind spot in human nature. Despite knowing that the world is changing every day, people are not aware that they should actively change themselves. Rooted habits are a great obstacle to change.

Thirdly, religions do not always tell all the truth. They use a number of rituals and other methods to eliminate the negative impact of meat eating and the true problem of so-called 'humane slaughtering'. Thousands of years ago, the Chinese Taoist practitioners said 'clean' intestines could lead to a healthy and long life. Not until recently did the scientific community verify that the intestinal tract is like the second brain – it can receive, record and convey messages. Common sense tells us there is an obvious difference between meat-based diet and plant-based diet. One usually feels heavy after eating meat but feels lighter and more relaxed after eating a plant-based meal. This is because after eating meat-based food, more adverse intestinal chemicals are produced which can sometimes cause indigestion. A vegetarian who has eaten a balanced diet over a long period of time, has a relatively clean intestinal tract and is better able to relax. Reducing the burden on the intestine is fundamental. Before we purify our body, mind and spirit, we should start by eating 'clean' food first. In summary the difference between meat-based and vegetable-based diets is the difference in mental and physical results each diet produces.

An experiment was conducted in the prisons of Taiwan where the prisoners' diet was changed from a meat-based one to a vegetarian one. This shift resulted in a positive change in the inmates' behaviour. Doctors and nurses of the Christian Sabbath Church in Taiwan have observed that vegetarian patients recover significantly faster from surgery than meat-eating patients.

Finally, another significant factor which impedes the promotion of vegetarianism is that people usually believe that a solely plant-based diet might result in malnutrition, forgetting that the athletic monks of the Shaolin Temple and elephants are both vegetarians. It is true that people who have eaten a meat-based diet for a long time will be more attached to the flavour of meat. It is also true that many people get a primal satisfaction from eating meat, their favoured expression being "no meat, no joy". Yet it is also true that cooking with Taoist simplicity and intelligence can easily create interesting combinations and bring out the natural flavours of the plant ingredients.

2,500 years ago, a saint in the East called Wei Mo Jay once said:

"One can enter Tao through eye, ear, nose, tongue, body and mind. Entering Tao through the tongue is truthful."

If cooking food could help us enter the state of Tao, spiritual and energy ascension, then our human society could return to simplicity, and enter the state of "getting along with nine clans in peace" (from the Book of History or Shang Shu). At such a time, the collective consciousness of humanity would be significantly raised and the ecological calamities we face would be reduced or eliminated.

New dishes on the table.
No more calamities!

New Garden City movement

| Philip Ross

| Former Mayor of Letchworth

The aim of the new Garden City movement is to revisit Ebenezer Howard's original vision of a Garden City and to determine what the criteria would be for defining, designing or designating what makes a Garden City, town, or community in the 21st century.

We are now over 100 years on from the original publication of his seminal book *Garden Cities of To-morrow* and the general public's general perception of Garden Cities is that it has something to do with a certain style of architecture and green spaces. Elsewhere it is considered some sort of historical oddity and even a form of 'heritage' to be preserved. When Howard wrote his book and when his first architects Barry Parker and Raymond Unwin were setting up their drawing boards, architecture was just a means to an end. The desired outcome was the creation of a sustainable community, one that would be in harmony with itself and with the countryside that surrounded it.

There are new cities being built throughout the world today and many of the architects will no doubt be inspired by some of the original Garden City design ideas. Some are innovating for the 21st century and are focusing on low-carbon models and are vying to be 'green cities': such as Tianjin in China and Masdar in Abu Dhabi. Such efforts are to be applauded and commended. Yet, is achieving a zero-carbon status policy all that is needed to be a 21st century Garden City?

We think that such strides and ambitions are important but they are not the only ones that could make a 21st century Garden City. Howard's vision, which we share, and which was shared by reformers, designers and activists throughout the 20th century, was a city where its citizens would have a common purpose through a shared set of progressive values and principles. People living in Garden Cities would be citizens of their town, not subjects of their landlord, however well meaning or benevolent they might be.

Citizenship has always been defined through access to land and the same is true today. Feeling part of the city and the community in which you live is a key manifestation of citizenship. It is a reciprocal mixture of rights and responsibilities between the city and the citizen, with the citizen knowing that the wealth of the town is people that live in it and that the prosperity of the city will be shared. To understand this we need only look back into history both recent and past. For example, Ancient Rome was originally a republic of citizen farmers. To be a citizen you had to own land. Only by owning land would you have a stake in society. Similarly, democracy in Western Europe was for a long time linked to property qualification: how could you vote if you had no physical stake in society?

Anyone can build a town with houses, businesses and factories, but to build a sustainable community requires something extra that binds these together. This special ingredient is citizenship. Access to land and the ability to grow food in cities and urban areas is a key ingredient in nurturing this sense of citizenship; it is not just about growing food, it is in part about the right and power to do so. This may sound far removed from the comfort of the English home counties. But it should be a right as natural as that of collecting rainwater. Ironically, only a few years ago in Bolivia, a US-backed company made it illegal for people to collect rainwater without a permit. The short-term result was an uprising which was put down with brute force by the then incumbent President of Bolivia, Hugo Banzer. One of the results of this was the election of the socialist President Evo Morales in 2006.

While we are not suggesting that growing plants and potatoes is a political act in itself, the freedom to do so is the result of previous political acts. Growing food locally contributes to sustainability of the city and fits like a glove with Howard's view that a Garden City should bring the best of town and country together. While communal or personal gardens may not always be possible in a particular city or neighbourhood, aspiring to the appellation of 'Garden City' should encourage policies to be put in place such that unused land is reclaimed and allowed to be used for urban agricultural purposes. Part of the benefit of urban agriculture is that people come together in shared activity, which results in healthy produce, good health, and an increased sense of community.

The freedom to grow food is linked with citizenship and a feeling of place, equality and purpose. It is for this reason that the ability to access land within the city for growing food through allotments or other mechanisms is an essential part of any Garden City.

One hundred and sixty eight venison pasties

I Sarah Ann Milne

I School of Architecture and the Built Environment, University of Westminster

A stones-throw away from the Bank of England, buried below ground in a small archive room (peculiarly accessed through a hidden door at ground floor level), a special place is reserved for a document referred to as the *'Dinner Book'*.

With so many records destroyed in the Great Fire of London, this fascinating document appears unique in its age, breadth, consistency and detail describing Tudor feasting practices in the City. It meticulously records the cost, content and management of the annual Election Day Feasts of the Drapers Company for the period 1564-1602 in extraordinary detail. Through the exacting nature of the costs, payments for servants and products, the book offers insights into the social, familial and spatial make-up of the Elizabethan City in full-flow.

From beginning to end, through the gifting of food, it seems the feast was a tangible demonstration of corporate patronage and generosity. Through the gifting of food, honour could be gained and maintained through the public representation of commitment and support to those both socially superior and inferior. For example, in preparation for the feast, hunting gifts of 40 male deer were gifted to the Company by individuals. And yet, despite feeding 89 guests, and 53 servants, on Sunday, Monday and Tuesday, enough meat was left over to produce 168 pasties! This was no meagre feast.

Amusingly, an entire chapter of the documentation of the 1564 feast is devoted to the creation and distribution of venison pasties made from the leftover meats. The careful allocation of each one of these was clearly a matter of concern for the note-taking clerk; like Samuel Pepys, perhaps he had a particular penchant for venison pasties and bemoaned his own rather measly one pasty.

Just what was so special about these pasties anyway? Having been served to the social elite of London at the 'High Table' of the feast, these pasties would have been ornately decorated and very large (wholly unlike today's handheld pasties). The text indicates a whole haunch of venison would have been baked in such a pasty. The tough rye-based pastry ensured the precious meat inside remained succulent and tender, while the outer shell was resilient enough to be easily transported without cracking. Often referred to as 'cofyns', the outer pastry would typically not have been eaten, discarded for the meat inside (spooned out after breaking through the patterned lid). The delivery of these miniature embodiments of the feast would surely have been entertaining: carts overflowing with pasties

slowly making their way around the city streets pushed by harassed porters.

Notably, after allocating pasties to servants, small businesses, taverns frequented by the Company, family, neighbours, and other notable persons unable to attend due to infirmity, the Drapers turned to serve the City poor. It had, by this time, become tradition for paupers to loiter by the hall gates in the realistic hope that they might receive remnants from the feast. Fifteen pastries were donated 'to the Neighbours afore our gate' in 1564. Meanwhile, at the other end of the scale a special delivery was dispatched to the home of 'Mister Lord Lloyd George', who, in addition to his pasty, also received a large sampling of the finest food at the feast. And all this to be delivered by one of the most 'handsom' servants available. Clearly, he was one to impress...

In this way, the episode of the 168 venison pasties reveals more than a grumbling clerk who (understandably) enjoys his leftovers. Instead, we begin to see the Drapers' ambition for honour being worked out intimately across all the levels of City society through the informal process of food exchange.

Organiclea

| Khadija Gitay

The river Lea flows between Hertfordshire and London, forming the Lea Valley which is an ideal site for growing crops. In the 6th century AD, the Saxons were the first people who settled and worked the land, followed by the Danes in around 894 AD.

The Danes grew the same type of crops as the Saxons: oats, wheat, rye, leaks, celery, carrots and beans. Importantly, the Danes established the first market garden on the site. It was the use of the River Lea to transport grains from the countryside to London which prevented Londoners from dying of hunger during the Great Plague. By the 17th century, Lower Lea was famous for its market gardens and exotic fruit growing.

In the 19th century, allotments were established at Markhouse and Higham Hill Common, both in Walthamstow. These are believed to be the second oldest working allotments in London. In 1930, the production of tomatoes in the Valley alone was worth over half of the total agricultural produce of the entire country. During World War Two, Lea Valley food production reached its peak under the government-led campaign 'Dig for Victory'. Shortly after the war, Scandinavian and Dutch people moved to the area to work in the glasshouses.

Although the 2012 Olympics has changed the face of the Lower Lea by removing the most beautiful allotment site – Manor Garden Allotments – it has not prevented food growing from taking place along the Lea banks and further afield as part of a growing movement to 'reclaim the fields'.

In 2007 the Council-run Hawkwood Plant Nursery was closed down. Inspired by the rich food-growing heritage of the Lea Valley, an employee of the nursery took the opportunity to continue with the legacy of the site – and the area – by developing an urban food growing enterprise on the same site. After a long negotiation with the local Council, Organiclea were granted a ten year lease to use 12 acres of land in 2010. Organiclea is a workers' cooperative based in Chingford, Waltham Forest. Crops grown on the plant nursery site are sold at the Hornbeam Café, a local community centre, or via a box scheme with seasonal fruits and vegetables being delivered to the surrounding neighbourhoods.

Organiclea adopts a holistic approach by creating a localised food system that can help improve local residents' quality of life, while at the same time tackling issues such as health, environmental and social justice and fairness. Organiclea is predominantly made up of volunteers, who are given a share of the crops they help grow, with a small number of part-time staff. At present, the Council has only charged a subsidised rate to reduce operational costs and support small scale farmers via crop share. In the long run, Organiclea aims to be financially independent in the next few years and win over permanent land tenure from the Council.

Unlike standard English farming systems which rely on animal manure as fertilizer, Organiclea uses a stock-free, or animal free, growing system. A number of the cooperative members are vegan so they practice a growing philosophy that reflects this. Green manure, as a replacement for animal manure, is a gentler way of increasing fertility of the soil. Animal manure has to be allowed to decompose over a period of time, otherwise the raw animal manure can scorch plants roots and destroy the plants.

Volunteering at Organiclea brings back a lot of childhood memories. I was brought up in India around many people who grew their own food. My grandmother used to grow runner beans, coriander and spinach. She would let certain plants go to seed then carefully dry them and store the seeds for the next season. I was also aware that when she grew spinach in the shade the leaves tasted bitter. All these small tips I learned as a child have influenced the way I appreciate and value food today. I am pleased to see more children involved in food growing in their school

or at home especially for those living in a big city like London. It is a challenge to grow your food in our densely populated urban environment. However, there are many opportunities available to us with community gardens, roof gardens and more and more public space being used to grow food.

Organiclea not only inherited the unique history and geography of the Lea Valley on London's urban edge, it has also demonstrated that growing food in an ecologically friendly, just and fair manner is desirable and practically possible. The multitude of initiatives which reconnect people with growing and celebrating sustainably grown food deliver a powerful message; reclaiming our food future means putting people and planet before the profits of agro-industrial and food processing companies.

Organiclea provides a model for rebuilding a localised food system which will help to restore a sense of meaning and belonging to the place we live. To end, I would like to share a quote by Noam Chomsky from Organiclea's blog:

"If you assume there's no hope, you guarantee that there will be no hope. If you assume that there is an instinct for freedom, there are opportunities to change things, there's a chance you may contribute to making a better world. That's your choice".

The soul of the Lea Valley is ideal for growing crops as well as our hopes.

Poetry menu

I **Simon Barraclough**

I Poet in the City

Pizza Heart

Squat ellipsoid of dough.
Yeasty, pummelled, elastic.
You knuckle into it,
it takes the dimpled kneading
of your need,
you twirl it thin and wide, ridiculous dervish.
Into the fire with it.
Delicious.

St. Francis of the Boston Hilton

surrendered all his worldly goods
to the check-in clerk (who held them till
his flight had left, then sent them down another path
to the belly of a plane to Belize).

Removed his coat and shoes, eschewed
the airline food and landed naked in the rain.
The least I could do was lend him my robe
and take him down to Legal Sea Foods.

No sooner had he sipped his sauvignon
than popcorn shrimp began to pop into his mouth,
pink lobsters propped on mermaid tails peered from their pots,
Alaskan King Crabs beat their shells like clockwork toys,

Atlantic Salmon curling on the grill
took one last glimpse before their eyes smoked dim,
then swam to sea through open gills.
That night the dishes cooked and served themselves,

the tables swayed beneath the mounting plate
and endless crates delivered cannonades of cork
and no one asked for, no one brought, nobody thought
to pick up the bill

Éclair de Lune

"Please tell me," said Madame, *"do poets like cake?"*
"Yes," replied Auden. *"Very much indeed."*

Journey to a War, Auden and Isherwood

You slide the bolt against the final diner.
Through the art-deco window, a moonbeam
pale as jasmine tea hits the Gaggia machine.

After all the chatter and rattle of china,
you kick off your shoes, move in to me,
bring your mouth's glazed-strawberry sheen.

I hike your apron with floury fingers
over thighs as slender as éclairs
and gently heft you onto the counter,

rolling your haunches in the debris
of icing sugar, almonds, leavened dough,
before dropping to my knees below

to free you from these workaday cares
as the moon slowly arcs out of the scene,
until the thud of newspapers shoos the dream.

138

Queen's Market curry

| Freek Janssens

| University of Amsterdam / Stil Novo

From the moment that the production of food became separated from the consumption of it, both markets and cities emerged: they are two sides of the same coin.

Since food is such a crucial element in everyone's life, those who were in charge of the food supply were in charge of life and death – of the city and quite literally of its inhabitants. Local authorities derived legitimacy from their capacity to feed the city. No wonder that markets have historically been heavily managed and policed. As part of the London Plan – the Mayor of London's overall planning document – a food vision has been developed to influence the way food travels through the city.

When cities expanded and became more disconnected from the food producing hinterland, they also started to loose their grip on the food supply. The market principle of free and private trade took over from the principle of a public and state-controlled marketplace. Increasingly, it was the large, privately owned and internationally operating businesses, which fed the city and consequently, played an ever-growing role in ruling it. But who is in charge of these businesses?

There are still many markets scattered across London that are managed by local boroughs. Many of these markets are under threat. From Brixton in South West London to Seven Sisters in the north east, local councils are failing to understand the importance and see the hidden beauty of local markets. Financially constrained councils are tempted by high land prices to sell market spaces to private property developers.

Markets offer healthy and affordable food and provide accessible entrances into entrepreneurship and hence financial independence. Markets also boost the local economy and provide meaning and memory to neighbourhoods. Despite these benefits, local authorities are struggling to understand and appreciate their value.

One particular market that was neglected, and almost destroyed by Newham Council, was Queen's Market in Upton Park. Once called "a world on a plate", London's most ethnically diverse market brings together people, food, and ideas from all over the world. Queen's Market opens up to all the continents through its staggering range of products. As my friend told me, his mother's curry changed according to what she could find in Queen's Market that day. These curries embody the unique places that markets are: creative spaces that are open to all, truly universal, and at the same time absolutely personal. In the eyes of the Council however, Queen's Market is a dirty, unmanageable place.

Queen's Market curry:

Ingredients:
10 lamb chops
Small orange pumpkin
2 onions
A few cloves of garlic
Small stick of ginger
Handful of coriander
A few chillies
Mild curry powder

To make:
Cook a base of 2 onions in olive oil, a few pieces of finely chopped garlic and ginger, salt and pepper. Allow to completely soften. Add 2 tablespoons of mild curry powder, mixing contents into a paste. Add 10 lamb chops. Let the meat cook in the paste, colouring the meat until almost frying it. Add a little hot water if needed. After the meat has gained some colour add a few cups of hot water, cover the pan with lid on a medium-slow heat. Let the meat cook slowly in the curry sauce. Meanwhile add some finely chopped chillies to the pan. Cut a peeled orange pumpkin into pieces and add to the pan. Stir content, cover and let simmer. Finally add finely chopped coriander. After 30-45 minutes of simmering you have soft sweet pumpkin mixed in a rich lamb chop curry.

A supermarket, they argue, is much more manageable. Who wouldn't want a supermarket?

Yet, supermarkets are sterile places, which offer the same produce every day. Their profit, rather than going into the local economy, goes to unknown investors. Contrary to a 'real' marketplace, like Queen's Market, supermarkets are places where there is only one concept, one structure – order rules in supermarkets, and chaos is not allowed.

Markets are able to relate creatively to the universal and the personal simultaneously, which are useful starting points for addressing the problems of our time. Rather than hiding behind large supermarkets, local authorities should support and promote their markets. Hopefully, London will set an example by recognising the value of markets in the 2011 Replacement London Plan[1].

[1] The London Plan., available at (http://www.london.gov.uk/shaping-london/london-plan/) (accessed 29 June 2011)

Quite nicely

Christopher Benstead

garlic, On a low heat (toss 'em if you can) Now baste the ha-llou-mi with some

good o-live oil, Place the sli-ces on your ba-king tray (You could use some foil if you like) Keep an

eye on your grill, We want sli-ces gol-den brown on ei-ther side, Chop some mint and ba-sil (or use your

sea-son-ing of choice) Add the herbs to the sa-lad And a squeeze of le-mon juice, It'-ll make it all taste

nice-ly, Quite nice-ly Now pour in the mush-rooms With the gar-lic and the juice (It'-ll

give a nice fla-vour to the leaves that you've used) Now, take your ha-llou-mi from be-

neath the grill, Place the pie-ces on top of the sa-lad (Add some gra-ted pe-pper if you will) And your

warm yu-mmy sa-lad is all rea-dy to be served with a nice glass Of le-mon-ade to quench the thirst of your

guests, And the rest is all up to you To en-ter-tain as you wish With an an-ec-dote or

two, That'-ll do, quite nice-ly, Quite nice-ly It will su-ffice-ly It's cheap at the

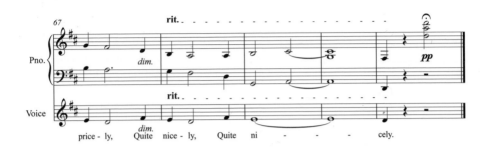

price - ly, Quite nice - ly, Quite ni – – – cely.

Reclaiming land

I **Dr. Ian Fitzpatrick**

Take a wildly unequal land distribution problem (in the UK, 0.3% of the population own 69% of the land).

Combine this with rising land and food prices, decreasing national food self-sufficiency (down 10% in the last decade), falling farm incomes, rapidly declining numbers of farmers (293,000 people working on farms as of 2010 – a 12% drop from the year 2000) and continuous talk of global food (in)security. Stir. Add climate change (described by the World Economic Forum as "the greatest challenge facing humanity this century") and rising fuel prices. Include (optional): the fact that the owners of between 30% and 50% of all the land in the UK are not recorded on the land registry; and that huge subsidies from the EU and UK encourage large land-owners to simply sit on unproductive land. The result is an intractably unsustainable and deeply precarious food and farming system; i.e. an urgent problem to be solved with a different kind of logic to the one that created it.

A life on the land ignites the imagination and idealism of countless uprooted and rootless urban dwellers: witness the huge allotment waiting lists. But this yearning goes deeper than a few hours of digging and weeding on a sunny Saturday. It is about creating and valuing land-based livelihoods in a country with less than 1% of the population involved in agriculture. It is also fundamentally about developing tight-knit, resilient and sustainable communities able to provide most of their own resources and services (London has an 'ecological footprint' over 200 times its own size).

Paths towards a rekindled rural (and to some extent urban and peri-urban) economy have already been partly cleared. CSA allows farmers and a local community to support each other and share the benefits and risks of food production. Community Land Initiatives such as Fordhall Farm, make farmers the tenants on land owned by a community group. Land Partnerships (e.g. Landscope) occur when landowners

lease part of their land to small farm enterprises in a mutually beneficial arrangement. While these models serve as useful examples of what is possible, and interest in them continues to increase, it is hard not to feel pessimistic about their potential for wider diffusion. So many obstacles stand in the way – cultural, financial and legal constraints – and their current contribution to food production and land use seems like little more than a drop in the ocean.

Another possible path to a rekindled rural economy is that of reclaiming abandoned, derelict, unused land for community-based food growing projects. Such reclaiming can also take a more defiantly political tack and be used as a physical expression of the need for a reorientation or re-examination of land use. Members of the Landless Workers' Movement (MST) in Brazil, have regularly targeted land owned by multinational corporations in protest at what are considered unjust and unsustainable land use practices. In the UK, food growers, activists and members of the local community took over an abandoned nurseries site on land originally earmarked for Heathrow airport's third runway. 'Grow Heathrow' is now a vibrant community food growing project in the shadow of Europe's largest airport. It is examples such as these, combined with the experiences of small-scale farmers, CSA and land partnership projects, which serve as a useful map (or menu) of paths to a more just and sustainable food and farming system.

Pickled blackberry leaf buds:

This is a useful recipe for any land reclaimer. Creeping brambles are among the most ubiquitous plants on abandoned farm land.

Ingredients:

80 (approximately) blackberry leaf buds – peeled shoots can also be used
3 cups of cider vinegar
½ cup of sugar or honey
1 tsp black peppercorns
1 tsp coriander seeds
1 cinnamon stick
2 dried chillies (optional)
2 bay leaves
1 tbsp of salt

To make:

Take the leaf buds (which look like tight bundles of leaves on new stems) or shoots (peeled and cut at 10cm intervals) and place them in boiling water for 5 minutes. Change the water and repeat. This helps to remove some of the bitterness. Drain the buds and place them together with the remaining ingredients in a large jar. Top-up with vinegar to make sure all the buds are covered. Leave in a dark place for 3-4 weeks. Pickled buds have a light nutty flavour and taste great on oatcakes.

Reclaiming waste

I Sara Wingate Gray

I Department of Information Studies, UCL

Food and drink is big business. The annual estimated market for UK food and food services just to the public sector is worth more than £2 billion, with UK household expenditure estimated at £95.1 billion.

The 2010 DEFRA Food Statistics Pocketbook[1] estimates that of the 11.3 million tonnes which constitute waste in the UK household supply chain, 8.3 million tonnes is food waste alone.

More than 60% of this food and drink household waste was in fact fit to be consumed at some point prior to its disposal. This means that of the 8.3 million tonnes added to the food waste chain by UK households, 5.3 million tonnes of this food would have been able to be eaten if better food management in the home had taken place, including appropriately dealing with leftovers (defined as food and drink prepared and/or served but not consumed), and food and drink disposed of due to it

not being used in a timely fashion (defined as either passing a use-by date, or going mouldy)[2].

Food waste is a difficult subject, not least because outcomes of methods of collection, reclamation, recycling, and disposal in this process can generate further 'waste' products themselves (such as greenhouse gas emissions from, for example: burning of fossil fuels for transportation; use of nitrogen fertiliser in agriculture; emissions from cattle).

Dealing with waste, and food waste in particular, is therefore an especially difficult process, but I'd like to suggest that one of the underlying problems to finding a solution here is that our understanding may be being masked by the definitions and terminology that are in use. The definition of 'waste', according to the United Nations Statistics Division is: "materials that are not prime products (that is products produced for the market) for which the generator has

Figure 1: Breakdown of UK household food and drink purchases, which enter the food waste process.

[1] DEFRA Food Statistics Pocketbook 2010. (http://tinyurl.com/DEFRApocketbook)

[2] Household Food and Drink Waste in the UK; November 2009. (http://tinyurl.com/WRAP2009), (accessed May 2011)

no further use in terms of his/her own purposes of production, transformation or consumption, and of which he/she wants to dispose".

For me, this definition demonstrates some of the fundamental assumptions and limits in thinking that occur when we only think of waste in this way, particularly since 'one woman's waste is another woman's treasure'. That is to say, this definition only allows for the fact that if the producer of 'waste' deems it as such, then that is what it becomes, thus entering the waste management chain without further discussion. However, it is entirely possible that what is viewed as 'waste' by the instigator of production may in fact be viewed as 'product' or 'consumable' or 'valuable' by another.

Here, I speak from direct experience of investigating the amount of food determined as 'waste' by a number of supermarkets in three different countries, spending time essentially going through the garbage bins to collect food products deemed by these supermarkets as 'waste'. In London, San Francisco, and Leipzig, I saw first-hand the amount of food being 'wasted' in this way, which specifically included:

- Fruit in cotton net bags where one item has become inedible and because of selling practices, the whole bag must be removed and deemed waste.
- Pre-packaged fruit, which has been sliced up for 'convenience', has a

much more limited shelf-life and therefore more quickly becomes a waste product if left unsold. 'Ready meals' also fall into this category.

• Vegetables which have reached their 'sell-by' date, but which are still entirely edible must be thrown out due to working and legal practices.

These are just a few examples of the many products entering the food waste chain via supermarkets every day of the week across individual towns and cities spanning the entirety of Europe and North America. What was most disturbing to me in this investigation was the actual quality of food that was deemed to be worthy of definitions of 'waste', as in almost every bin I investigated I found food products entirely edible, in some instances without blemishes, mould or broken surfaces at all. Most shocking of all, the quantity of 'food waste' available in this way meant that for several months at a time I was able to live entirely from reclaiming this produce.

Of course, there are no quick and easy solutions to this issue, and I would not like to suggest that the answer is simply to encourage everyone to nip behind their local supermarket every evening post-midnight and launch themselves into a green, blue or brown bin. Instead, what I'd like to introduce is the idea that to solve these issues we need to change our practices to engage more fully with the concepts of sharing, which also involve the notions of re-use, reclamation and recycling, and I take the Public Li-

brary sector as inspiration here, engaging as it does with the ideas of recycling and re-use via the very public process of lending, borrowing, and re-using of 'products' and 'information', a streamlined process which occurs in public libraries across the UK every day.

Instead of introducing these concepts to the food waste cycle we are allowing a destructive short-term approach to drive the way the process operates, whereby much "of the activity undertaken by retailers regarding their food waste so far seems to have focussed on landfill diversion rather than waste prevention"[3], with the result that further waste and costs are generated, not less.

Ultimately, of course, a large part of the food waste dilemma, as the statistics have shown us, also comes down to us as individuals in the households we live in. Next time you're in the supermarket or your local outdoor market, or indeed your kitchen, spend some time thinking about how you can reduce what you waste. As one contributor to the food waste chain might say, every little helps.

[3] Waste Arisings in the Supply of Food and Drink to UK Households; March 2010, pg5. (http://tinyurl.com/WRAP2010)

Bruschetta: dumpster-style:

All ingredients found in two bins at the back of a supermarket in Leipzig, 2009 – you'll have to be prepared to improvise if you try to make this in the same way that I have, as often the best bit of food bin rummaging is that you never know what you're going to find and therefore get to eat!

Ingredients:

Bread of some sort
Green and red bell peppers
Cherry tomatoes or plum tomatoes
- ideally a mix of both
Olive oil and balsamic vinegar,
Salt and pepper
2 cartons of red wine
Fresh leaves from a basil plant
Red onion
Garlic

To make:

Pre-heat the oven to 230°C. Prepare the vegetable ingredients: first chop and cut your peppers and tomatoes finely. Remove the seeds from your peppers before chopping, and you can remove the seeds and juice from the tomatoes too (but I like to keep them). Slice and dice your garlic and red onion.

While you are waiting for the oven to reach the correct temperature, put the peppers, tomatoes, garlic, onion, oil and vinegar in a bowl and give them a good mix. This is also a good time to open the wine and give it a taste!

Chop the basil leaves as finely as you can be bothered and add to your previous mix. Add salt and pepper to taste.

Slice whatever bread you've found on a diagonal into about 1/2 inch thick slices. Coat one side of each slice with olive oil and then toast them (olive oil side down) until golden brown.

Place bread oil side up in a dish and then evenly spread the vegetable and herb mix onto each slice, adding a nice drizzle of oil after.

Serve with a whole basil leaf on top or on the side of the plate for decoration. Top up your wine now and enjoy!

Rediscovering the sacred

I Susie Weldon

I Faith in Food Programme

It's impossible to separate food from faith. Food plays a key role in religion, whether in worship, as in the sharing of bread and wine that is at the heart of the Christian mass, or as part of a faith-consistent lifestyle, as in the rules around what is kosher, or fit to eat, that have governed Jewish diets for nearly 3,000 years.

Every faith celebrates food as a gift of the Divine and every faith shares an understanding of social justice. As the Prophet Mohammed urged his followers: "Give food to the hungry, pay a visit to the sick and release the one in captivity."

Food, or the growing of food, is often used as a metaphor in religious texts. Consider these beautiful lines from Bahá'u'lláh, Prophet-Founder of the Bahá'í religion:

"Hearken to the delightsome words of My honeyed tongue, and quaff the stream of mystic holiness from My sugar-shedding lips. Sow the seeds of My divine wisdom in the pure soil of thy heart, and water them with the water of certitude, that the hyacinths of My knowledge and wisdom may spring up fresh and green in the sacred city of thy heart."

In fact, food is so commonplace in religious ritual, symbol and practice that, ironically, many of us have lost sight of its sacred value. Harvest festivals no longer have the significance for today's supermarket generation that they did for people whose survival depended on what they produced from the land. We're also less devout; how many of us remember to thank God for our meal before tucking in?

Yet, in recent years, growing numbers of people have been rediscovering a sense of the sacred in food and building a new relationship with what they eat, based on their religious values. This movement of faith-consistent eaters is driven by an understanding that if we believe this world was created by God, we have a responsibility to care for it. And of all our daily choices, decisions around food are the most powerful. Eating is a moral act; our choices of what, when and how we eat have a huge impact upon the Earth, our fellow human beings and other living creatures.

Agriculture influences the way half the world's habitable land is cared for and two-thirds of the world's fresh water is used. The intensification of agriculture in recent decades has dramatically boosted crop yields but at huge cost,

including soil degradation, water pollution, desertification, toxic chemical residues and vast swathes of forests chopped down to grow crops. What's staggering is the speed of the damage; the UN's Food and Agriculture Organization estimates that around 75% of the world's genetic diversity of domestic agricultural crops and livestock was lost in the last century alone.

Climate change and a ballooning world population predict a bleak future. Already one billion people go to bed hungry but the price of staple foods such as maize are expected to double in the next 20 years, leading to an era of permanent food crisis, according to Oxfam's alarming 2011 report, *Growing a Better Future*. We must find a way to feed ourselves without trashing the Earth. That's why the Alliance of Religions and Conservation launched its Faith in Food initiative in November 2010 as a global movement aimed at helping faith communities honour their values in the food they eat, grow and buy.

The ecological crisis is as much a crisis of the spirit as of the earth. By rediscovering a sense of the sacred in food, we may move a step closer to the state described by the ancient Hindu text, the *Chāndogya Upanishad*: "When one's food is pure, one's being becomes pure."

Rethinking your vegetables

I **Lesley Acton**

I UCL Institute of Archaeology

Allotments are small plots of rented land used for growing fruits and vegetables for personal consumption.

Allotments still conjure up images of old men tending to cabbages and the World War II Dig For Victory campaign, when the British population was encouraged to become as self-sufficient as possible in food production. However, behind these iconic public memories is a movement steeped in history, inextricably linked to the land and its people, and experiencing a worldwide renaissance today, lending it more relevance than ever. Concern for diet and health, a desire not to lose more urban green spaces and the need to work towards a zero carbon future have fuelled a renewed demand for allotments.

Allotments have always been credited with benefits above and beyond the production of food. In the nineteenth century, they were said to improve morals, reduce crime and make men better servants! Not everybody approved though. John Stuart Mill thought allotments were a 'method of making people grow their own poor rate,' since allotments were a way of reducing the Poor Law Tax for the landed classes. In the depression of the 1930s, they were said to keep men from suicide by giving them a purpose in life, and also to prevent and/or cure tuberculosis.

Nevertheless, the beginnings of the allotment movement are obscure. One movement (it seems there were several beginnings) appears to be connected with the largesse of eighteenth century northern industrialists, who provided their workers with gardens to grow their own food. In the early nineteenth century, allotments were provided to alleviate the distress of the rural poor and by the end of the century were made widely available in both rural and urban areas. Unfortunately, the number of allotments has dropped from a peak of about 1.4 million in World War II to about 300,000

today, but demand remains high and some areas of the country have 40-year waiting lists.

With the shortage of allotments, many innovative urban agricultural projects have sprung up. There are vegetable gardens in skips, which can be moved to new locations if their current sites are redeveloped or claimed for other purposes. All sorts of low/no-space areas have been reclaimed as vegetable plots. Roadside verges, rooftops, fire escapes, vertical structures that allow cultivation on walls, grow bags and plastic bottles are but a few ideas.

However, all this effort will come to nothing if we continue to waste food in the staggering quantities that we do. Of course, in the words of Webster[1], we 'do not wish to be condemned to eat cauliflowers day after day simply because it is their season, and they are clamouring for consumption.' Today though, unlike during Webster's time, we can freeze food. Nevertheless, not everything can be frozen. Carefully planned planting and regular sowing will help, but nature doesn't always oblige. Using different cultivars and transplanting seedlings (frequently) is one way of helping to prolong availability.

Without recourse to freezers and re-frigeration, how can we not waste what is grown? We can dry, bottle and pickle produce, swap and even sell it, but one long-forgotten tradition is to harvest vegetables at different times in their

Summer green soup:

Ingredients:
Cucumbers
Lettuces (stems of bolted lettuce are great)
A small potato (optional)
Onions

To make:
Sauté ingredients gently in a little butter and/or olive oil until soft. Add stock, season and blend.

Serve hot or chilled with crème fraiche, chopped chives and/or mint and a drizzle of homemade herb-infused oil.

life-cycle. Use radishes, spinach, beet and pea shoots in salads and stems of bolted lettuces and leaves of cauliflowers in a stir-fry, for example.

What we grow is not a separate entity from what we eat. Historically, they were one and the same thing, which should still be the case today.

[1] Webster, T., 1844. *An Encyclopaedia of Domestic Economy*, London

Save the pookato

| **John Braime**

| UCL Volunteering Services Unit

It's an orangey-grey vegetable, thin and gnarled, with strands on one end like a wispy beard, so that it more often than not resembles an elongated face. I've always supposed it to be a relative of the sweet potato, though my Grandfather claimed it was *sui generis*.

He told me that he'd been made the custodian of the vegetable by a clan of warrior-monks from the Himalayas, back in his explorer days. The monks had ceased to exist long ago, and one day so would he. As such, I was to be the inheritor of the secrets of the pookato.

It was quite a responsibility for a seven-year old.

The pookato's uniqueness – Grandfather claimed – lay in its intricate nervous system. If more than four were put in close proximity, they developed a sort of collective consciousness which could be communicated with via his patented Pookatronics system (a couple of electrodes, a simple Morse code transmitter and an oscilloscope). In recognition of their high levels of intelligence, he'd only ever eat them on special occasions, generally holidays of his own creation, like Saint Tortoise's Day or Rubidium Thursday. Then, he'd bake five of the pookatoes, three for himself and two for me, and place them on the table with pots of butter and some shredded sage. We'd stand and give the pledge:

'Hail, wise vegetable. We promise to be worthy of your sacrifice.'

Next, we donned our navy blue smocks (this is what the Himalayan monks had worn) and put on the special hat, not unlike a deer-stalker wrapped in tin foil (which ensured that the pookatoes couldn't exert undue mental influence upon us). Only then could we tuck into our meal.

At the time, none of this seemed odd; it was just the sort of thing my Grandfather did. Like setting up a zoo populated entirely by out-of-work actors in monkey suits and pantomime horse outfits. Or establishing a new religious system based upon a close numerological analysis of the works of Dick Francis, and then excommunicating himself. Or self-publishing those books about plant reproduction, complete with alarming – and scientifically inaccurate – illustrations. My Grandfather was a sensible man who knew precisely what he was doing.

He died last year. Shortly afterwards, a bundle of documents arrived from his solicitors, bestowing upon me the title

of "Custodian of the Pookato", along with a three volume set of instructions, a pack of seeds, and a fully functioning Pookatronics kit.

"But people need to treat them with respect."

"I think you'd better take that up with our head office."

Since receiving the bundle, I've set up a colony of pookatoes in my greenhouse. I follow the instructions to the letter, only eating them on the designated dates, and performing the rituals as he meticulously described. I've shared this knowledge with just one friend, inducting her in accordance with section 245 of the instructions. I trust her entirely; she can't be the source of the leak.

Therefore, I can't understand why this supermarket has started selling them.

I came here last week, and there in the section put aside for the more exotic vegetables – that little quarantine zone of *taro, mooli*, etc. – lay a basket of pookatoes. They were unmistakable, not just for their distinctive appearance, but also because of the sign next to them saying 'New superfood – the pookato.'

There was a small explanatory leaflet, saying how they were rich in selenium and Vitamin A and high in fibre, as if they were an ordinary vegetable. I tracked down the store manager, but he didn't want to listen to the story of my Grandfather. Head office had sent him a batch as a trial, they'd been a steady seller.

I did, and I got nowhere. Emails have gone unanswered, phone calls unreturned. I've noticed another supermarket has started selling them, and some health food stores.

So here I am, each and every Saturday, sharing the secret with everyone. It's best that I wear my special hat and my blue smock. I've condensed Grandfather's booklet as best I can into my own leaflet, to raise awareness of the history and special characteristics of the pookato, the correct way to grow and eat and respect the vegetable. And exhorting people not to connive in their commercial exploitation. It's degrading for them.

It's a pleasant way of spending the day, standing here, making new friends. My Grandfather didn't have a funeral, and there isn't a grave; he'd arranged for his body to be fed to the lions at a passing circus. As such, this is my way of remembering him.

Silent food

| Adeline Tay

| University of Melbourne

"There is no such thing as empty space or empty time. There is always something to see, something to hear. In fact, try as we may to make a silence, we cannot."

"Silence (is) depended upon for sounds to exist" (John Cage)

Food is often spoken of as vitality. A life force. Nourishing and enlivening. Visually exciting, palatally tasty. Less often however is it associated with sound, or the lack thereof. Silence.

Yet, for me, ingredients are the quiet heroes to the dish. They sit quietly – in fridges and cupboards, persevering as entities in an intransigent way. They just are. I think about the little packets of concentrated dried goods that patiently chill until called upon to explode with flavour. Or perhaps chance upon a forgotten carcass or bone, rendered of its meat at an earlier festivity.

This recipe brings together things from my childhood with things in the now. 'Recipe' is a word that I use very loosely. Porridge, a dish of uncertain ingredients in unquantifiable measures, has paradoxically always been that defining dish for me. Food is an interjection that splices time. There is no such thing as empty calories. Or silent killers. Food is.

So this recipe is also an amalgamation of memory, flavour and the what-is-available. Put to boil and bubble – a delicate dinner on a winter's evening.

Cantonese porridge (*congee*) :

Ingredients:

1 tablespoon vegetable oil
1 knob of ginger
Handful of dried *ikan bilis* (small dried anchovies used in Asian cooking)
100g unsalted raw nuts
Leftover bones for stock (ham bone/duck carcass/chicken carcass)

2 cups jasmine rice
1 tsp salt
1 tbsp vegetable oil

4-5 dried scallops
1 tbsp sesame oil
Coriander leaves for decoration

To make:

Stock

Lightly fry for a minute 1 tablespoon of vegetable oil in stockpot a knob of ginger and a large handful of dried *ikan bilis* (small dried anchovies used in Asian cooking). Allow it to colour but not brown.

Add unsalted raw nuts. Put into pot leftover bones for stock. Cover with water, and put to a boil. Let stock simmer for 2-3 hours to separate ingredients from stock.

Rice

Rinse jasmine rice. Add 1 tsp of salt and 1 tbsp of oil. Let it rest for at least half an hour.

Dried scallops

Pour hot water over the dried scallops. Break up the scallops as they soften.

Porridge

Combine rice, scallops and water, and stock in pot. Jiggle pot gently to even out the rice but do not stir. Allow medium fire until porridge starts to boil, reduce flame to small. Cover the pot with lid slightly open. Allow porridge to simmer at a whisper for at least an hour. The rice will first expand as it takes in water, and then start to break up till it melds with the stock. Add some boiling water if stock is insufficient. Add salt and white pepper to taste. Drizzle a tablespoon of sesame oil. Turn flame off and serve with some coriander leaves.

Silkworms and mulberry

| **Phil Paulo**
| Camley Street Natural Park

Less than a ten-minute walk from King's Cross-St. Pancras station, Zari enters an entirely different world.

The mixed patches of woodland, pond, marsh, grassland, meadow and fen, are squeezed into this little oasis, a local nature reserve known as the Camley Street Natural Park, created on former industrial land and sandwiched between Regent's Canal and the railway line complex. She enjoys wandering around the park to experience a closer contact with nature and always finding something new to learn and to think about.

This is an early summer afternoon. She discovers a small mulberry tree which was planted only few months ago. It will be some years before it reaches a suitable size for sitting under, and also a couple of years before it will fruit. She learns from a volunteer working at the park that there is an ancient mulberry which is in a state of collapse at the nearby Greville Place Nature Reserve in Camden. It's interesting to compare the new mulberry in Camley Street with the older generation which is twisted, fallen and heavily fruiting though hidden from view.

She has a fond childhood memory of the silkworms in China which she used to take home together with handfuls of mulberry leaves. The white, delicate

insects were her lovely little pets. It was fun to keep a few silkworms and watch them develop. She noticed how the hungry caterpillars munched away day and night and how silkworms are fussy about their food, and if it is not just right they can starve. Later she moved to London and found out most of the mulberry trees in the UK are black mulberries (*Morus nigra*). These trees are slow growing and highly prized for their juicy black fruit which are eaten by birds, woodland mammals and people alike. Then she realised that a silkworm is an even fussier feeder than she had thought as it will only feed on the white mulberry (*Morus alba*).

As a matter of history, there are quite a number of mature black mulberry trees in London as they were introduced mistakenly by King James I in 1608. The King wanted to produce his own silk and farm silkworms, so he thought that he would plant mulberry trees across London to encourage this. Unfortunately he was misinformed and planted the black rather than the white mulberry and as a result we are now gifted with many old and beautiful black mulberry trees which produce an abundance of enjoyable fruit but unfortunately no silkworms!

The mulberry-silkworm connection is a fascinating case of one species' complete dependence on another for its existence. How do silkworms know that they only need mulberry leaves? What's the secret that allows a larva to increase its size 10,000 times from birth? Why is it that humans cannot get enough nourishment from a diet of only one particular kind of green leaves like silkworms can? Silkworms are also the foundation of an industry that dates back over 4000 years to China and the domestication of this species for such a long period of time has made it very dependent on humans for survival. Does that mean silkworms could not survive in the wild without humans?

Even more fascinating is that Zari can contemplate these questions right in the middle of a man-made urban natural paradise, behind one of the busiest transport hubs in London. The embodied experience of nature in the city enriches her contemplation of the relationship between a plant, an insect and a human being; an example of our exploitation of plants, insects and the power of food. She might not have an answer to each of her questions, but is able to enjoy a bunch of mulberries which might do something good to help her continue her journey in a world of wonder.

Spice Caravan

| Spice Caravan catering co-op

"When it comes to food people don't see us as refugees or Muslim women, they just see us as Spice Caravan. "

People just assume we're all on benefits and don't want to work but obviously through Spice Caravan we've proved that this is not true. It has given us courage, and ambition, it's given us a chance to prove ourselves, that we can run a business, I think it's given people that positive feeling that they can do whatever they want to do.

Can a regular home cook sell food to the public? Is it easier to start a cooking business on your own or in a co-operative? Does it make a difference that it's a group of refugee women? These are some of the questions thrown up when a charity started a catering co-op with a group of refugee women.

Salusbury WORLD (Working on Refugees' Learning and Development), based at Salusbury Primary School in Queen's Park, London, aims to help refugee pupils and their parents. These parents ran food stalls for school fundraising events based on authentic recipes from their home countries. Encouraged by enthusiastic feedback about their food, 11 women from Somalia, Sudan, Eritrea and Morocco wanted to start a catering enterprise. We quickly raised £4,000 from Brent Council, secured the use of a domestic kitchen at

the school and put on business training for the whole group through the lottery-funded *Making Local Food Work*.

Five months later, the lure of a refugee-themed festival with 20,000 people attending was too tempting so we frantically bought equipment and planned how to cook outside. On that June Sunday we sold 500 meals from a stall on the South Bank and had arrived. In the year since then, Spice Caravan has become well known locally having cooked at about 50 one-off events, plus weekly at a Farmers' Market and for school staff. We particularly like that our Muslim group provided the food for the Jewish Food Festival, under the kosher supervision of a Rabbi.

How hard was the jump from domestic to public cooking? We never realised at the start how much work is involved in organising, running and planning - on top of the cooking. We're lucky that the local community rallied to provide free professional branding, design, catering and business consultancy. As new caterers we have to communicate and build a reputation but the need to present well is a major extra requirement to selling good, simple cooking.

Complying with food hygiene turned out to be fairly easy though we worried about it a lot. Finding customers has also been easy. They approach us through networking and word of mouth, because our food is different and people really like the taste, the women's personalities and the concept. Being consistently profitable is harder to achieve. We had gigs at the start when we earned £1 an hour. That's risen to between minimum wage and London Living Wage levels thanks in part to our fortune to have free rent, utilities and management support. I'm struck by the number of experienced caterers we meet who are tired and struggling financially and the contrast with fresh enthusiastic people starting out.

Organising and communicating within a group of about eight people has been difficult at times. It's a challenge to work together in a kitchen when none of us had worked in a restaurant before and with no fixed manager to set consistent procedures. Without a hierarchy there were more internal arguments in the group than might be expected, some that have threatened our future, as well as friendships and closeness. It would have been easier to have imposed, or much better developed together, more structure and system early on.

On the other hand, the social benefits of a group have been much greater. According to Sarah Reynolds, manager of Salusbury WORLD:

> "It's been extraordinary, and it's completely transformed Salusbury WORLD, it's transformed the school community, and it's transformed the perception of these women in the local community. They're so much more actively out there. There is an air of optimism, humour and confidence that we have never witnessed before"

The group is fantastic at supplying food anywhere, anytime. Being refugees makes it harder because members have less experience of Western working routines including punctuality and paperwork. On the other hand, we show huge determination and spirit despite heavy family responsibilities, study and childcare. For this group, whose skills and qualifications are often not recognised after becoming refugees, food has provided an outlet to work, earn, learn and become more active.

In the words of one of the Spice Girls, Ayan Hassan:

> "Every time you cook for people, people eat your food, appreciate it, you're happy. If we get that kind of business we'll see ourselves out of poverty ... one day maybe it'll come true, our dreams."

Spreading cocoa love

| Petra Barran
| Choc Star

People often ask me if
I've thought about having
a shop. They see me
bowling around in my
choc-mobile and imagine
that the next obvious,
conventional step would
be a bricks and mortar
establishment.

But to me this would obliterate what it
is about being at the helm of a chocolate van that is so compulsive. When I
am cloaked in the familiar layers of the
Choc Star world – pink neon-lit van,
churning and shaking choc from every

surface – it is as if I'm surrounded by a
perpetually shifting city narrative that
informs and is informed by the presence
of the van.

I came up with the idea to create a
chocolate van – a mobile chocolate
bar offering a menu of the brown stuff
served iced, baked, frozen and straight
up – one night in 2005. I wanted to take
good choc to the streets, to everyone;
anyone and whosoever might be passing by. I wanted to become a part of
the city that I had abandoned so freely
years before and I knew that chocolate
on wheels could give me that role. The
formula seemed so clear: chocolate
+ wheels + huge city = the potential to
meet a wonderfully diverse group of
people, to unite them under the universal arch of chocolate and then send
them on their way, back onto the streets
of London, all of us a little happier for it.

Out of the Choc Star window fly brownie
fudge sundaes cascading with warm
chocolate sauce, triple chocolate malted
milkshakes, super dark high-energy
truffles, Venezuelan hot chocolate
shots, and through the prism of all
this edible delight our world is viewed.
It takes place there and then, in front
of the customer. There they stand on
ground that is as much theirs as it is
ours; we all inhabit that same space and
are bonded for that moment by a kind of
co-production of the city. And as much
as London needs order and monitoring
it also desperately craves the ability to
react to chance and the unexpected.

Food sold in the open air gives a city a bit of funk in its right thigh. It helps to loosen up what Mike Davis has called the 'cold frozen geometries of the old spatial order' by injecting something everyone can partake of, whilst remaining enticingly ephemeral. I have been all over London in my choc-mobile. I've been to bar mitzvahs in Barnet and school playgrounds in Barking; I've peddled hot chocolate in Hounslow, and ice creams in Peckham. Every time I open the hatch it's a different face, a different story, but the smile and anticipation of pleasure remains unwaveringly, reassuringly the same. Though rootless, chocolate is my anchor and as I go 'all-city', London and its daily shifting populations make me feel a part of it, wherever I park.

Stirring up a storm of healthy habits

| Dr. Kate Evans, Charlene Shoneye
| Weight Concern

| Dr Laura McGowan, Susanne Meisel
| Health Behaviour Research Centre, UCL

In 2009, around three in ten boys and girls in England were classified as either overweight or obese[1]. Rates of obesity in the population have steadily increased over recent years and this trend is predicted to continue in the current environment[2].

Obesity increases the risk for many diseases such as diabetes, heart disease, and some cancers, as well as affecting quality of life and well-being. Unfortunately, obesity is now developing much earlier in life than it used to. Achieving and maintaining a healthy weight early in life is especially important because some of the negative health consequences of childhood obesity are irreversible.

Often, people blame the recent change in our living habits as the main cause for the obesity problem seen today. While this is partly true, it doesn't fully explain why some people are more likely to gain weight than others. Body weight, just as other characteristics such as height, or eye colour, has been found to be largely inherited. It has long been known that body weight runs in families, but it was difficult to establish whether this was due to genetic factors, or lifestyle factors, such as sharing the same family meals. Researchers in one study found that genes are responsible for about 70% of the differences in body weight between people[3].

However, this does not mean that the environment is unimportant. Humans evolved in an environment where feasts were infrequent and famines common. Therefore, our bodies developed ways to make the most of periods of plenty. These mechanisms are held in our genes. Their effects are responsible for factors related to eating, such as how we respond to the sight or smell of food, and how full we feel after eating. Differences in these genes can lead to people eating different amounts of food. When food is scarce, people with genes that encourage eating can thrive. In our current environment, where food is always available and the need for physical activity has been reduced, those whose genes make them more likely to gain weight are at increased risk of obesity. We must adjust our environment or the way we behave if we want to 'outsmart' any genetic tendencies to eat more than is good for us[4].

Childhood obesity presents a particular issue for society as we have a moral duty to care for children and protect them from harm. But weight remains a sensitive issue for many and knowing how to deal with the issue can be difficult.

As Benjamin Franklin once said: "An ounce of prevention is worth a pound of cure." Perhaps the key is getting in as early as possible. But how do we do this? By focusing on developing healthy habits early in life, the emphasis can shift away from weight itself, and towards positive, practical steps for change. Researchers have tested many different ways to promote healthy behaviours in children. Here is a selection of the most effective strategies for creating healthy habits:

- Parental food choices can strongly influence children's preferences, so it is important for the whole family to make healthy choices together.
- Tiny tastes of new or even disliked fruits and vegetables help to increase children's 'liking' of these foods, so be persistent.
- Encourage and praise positive eating behaviours such as trying new foods or making healthy choices.
- Avoid using food or drink as a reward; verbal praise, stickers, or rewards charts do better.
- Out of sight out of mind! Children are more likely to ask for food they can see. Have fruit and vegetables available for healthy snacks and keep the less healthy snacks and drinks out of the home except on special occasions.

- Turn off the TV and get active! Eating in front of the TV can reduce your child's ability to sense when they have eaten enough. Instead, eat meals as a family where possible, then the food can be fully enjoyed.

Developing healthier eating and activity habits early in life is positive for health and wellbeing. Strategies like those outlined here will help towards reversing the obesity epidemic we face. We want a future where children willingly choose the healthy option and are given an opportunity to be active.

[1] The NHS Information Centre, Lifestyles Statistics. (2011) Statistics on obesity, physical activity and diet: England, 2011.

[2] Must A, Strauss R.S., Risks and consequences of childhood and adolescent obesity. *International Journal of Obesity Related Metabolic Disorders* 1999;23:S2–11.

[3] Stunkard AJ, Foch TT, Hrubec Z. A twin study of human obesity. *JAMA* 1986;256:51-54.

[4] Can Exercise Trump Genetics? Times Online. ←http://tinyurl.com/57ub39→ accessed 08/09/2008.

Stolen honey

| Alison Benjamin and Brian McCallum
| Urban Bees

The label on our very first batch of honey read "STOLEN, honey from the hive in Alison's garden, Queen's Park, London, W9, Summer 2006".

It was designed to raise awareness that honeybees make honey for themselves. It is their winter stores in the hive; the carbohydrate they need to eat during the long cold months when there are few plants yielding the nectar they collect and turn into honey, and when the weather is too inclement for the bees to leave home in search of food.

As beekeepers we encourage our bees to make honey surplus to their winter requirements which we can then harvest for our own pleasure. Nevertheless, whatever we remove can still be classified as theft, hence the word we chose to display on those first few honey jars. We soon learnt, however, from the reaction of friends and family, when we joyfully gave away our amber-coloured liquid as birthday presents or dinner party gifts, that most people were uncomfortable receiving anything emblazoned with the term STOLEN, especially in capital letters.

The following batch and every batch thereafter has instead carried a very different home-made label, that aims to convey a sense of nostalgia and wellbe-

ing, and of bringing nature into the city with a childlike drawing of a hive and bees reminiscent of the famous E.H. Shephard *Winnie the Pooh* illustrations.

All that remains of the STOLEN honey is one jar kept for posterity. It sits on a shelf on the top of our book case in the front room. It is the first of some 35 small jars that are side by side in date order, chronicling our honey history since that hot summer six years ago. Some are palest straw, others deep amber, some are still as runny as the day we spun the honey off the comb, a few have crystallised and gone hard. Each has a label with the date the honey was harvested, where the hive was located and a batch number. Queen's Park honey is superceded by Battersea honey, after the bees and myself moved south to live with Brian in 2008. It is joined on the shelf by jars of Wallington honey, after my parents kindly agreed to host a couple of hives at the bottom of their large suburban garden, and King's Cross honey from the Urban Bees teaching apiary located on the edge of the London Wildlife Trust's green oasis in Camley Street. The latest addition is a pale, thin honey with a green tinge made by bees from the Museum of London. Theirs is the first offering from eight hives located across the square mile as part of the City of London Festival 2010.

The different consistencies, aromas and flavours of your honey depend on which combination of flowers are in bloom and have been visited by your bees. Urban honey is polyfloral because of the rich variety of flowers in gardens, parks, railway sidings and growing on bits of wasteland. But you can sometimes detect strong differences in flavour according to the dominant nectar source at different times throughout the summer. The Museum's green-tinged variety with a slight citrus taste will have come from the lime trees that flower in June and grace many a London street. Frequent visits to the horse chestnut tree will give your bees' honey a darker colour and hint of toffee. But unless you have a very sophisticated palate, it is difficult to decipher many of the other subtle variations.

For many urban apiarists, keeping bees at the bottom of the garden, on the roof, or on the allotment is a way of feeding their family locally-produced, unadulterated honey all year round. It is part of a drive for self-sufficiency and a personal crusade against the stranglehold the supermarkets have on our food supply. Although it won't save you any money, it is more rewarding to harvest honey from your hive than to pluck an anonymous jar from a supermarket shelf. For city dwellers like ourselves who had become totally divorced from how our food is produced, keeping bees has also made us appreciate what it takes to make this golden liquid that has been revered for millennia for its medicinal and culinary qualities, and has connected us with nature on our doorstep.

Student potential energy

| Christabel Buchannan

The growing problem: the most highly educated people in the Western world are not fulfilling their potential.

The number of university students is rising, but so is their reputation for disruption and lack of respect for their surroundings. In some university towns they are perceived as noisy, materially wasteful and socially segregated. In brief, they appear to take more than they give back to the wider community.

There are several issues at hand. First is the anonymity of city living and the distancing of people from the source of their food through greater urbanisation and global trade networks. Food has lost significance amongst younger people. A more central matter to students is that of temporality in location and status which makes the consequences of their actions a low priority. Outside of plugging career prospects, why would they establish relationships or implement creative ventures that they will eventually leave behind? Yet there is potential for a vision of sustainable living which involves gluing together communities and melting the hostilities between permanent city dwellers and students passing through.

The budding potential: The timing is crucial. Newly-found independence after flying away from the parental nest comes inevitably with lessons to be learnt. Although far from a homogenous group, students are characterised as being spirited and eager to learn. If students' energies were used collectively, and their spontaneity and sociability wisely, their impact would be durable and far-reaching. Student energy currently spent on short-term personal goals could be turned into something which benefits neighbourhoods, strengthens social ties and regenerates innate awareness of ecological sustainability for the future. All this starts in the back garden.

The field study: The solution lies in the cooperative use of land. Based on research carried out in a student area in Bath, launching a community garden share project would utilise abandoned space and give green-fingered residents space to grow food. Results so far have been promising. Relationships formed around food have been fundamental to transforming private spaces into thriving hubs of cooperative activity.

Tilling and toiling: The idea is simple, though in practice obstacles would emerge. Landlords are the most stubborn elements of this equation, but permission would be granted more readily as the scheme gains recognition. Concurrently, this idea would be planted into the mind of the wider community and garden share teams would spring up spontaneously. How tasks, practical and administrative, are divided up requires negotiation: gardening, seed and tool sharing balanced with distributing the edible rewards would need to be doled out fairly. Free food would incentivise student efforts. A core team would kick start the initiative and an online forum would make matching gardeners with gardens easy.

The collective green dream: This project offers a fresh vision of the future where space is too precious to waste; where shared knowledge and self-sufficiency are made into indispensible lifestyle assets for creating sustainable ways of eating and thinking locally. Inter-generational and inter-group dialogue will pay off in terms of skill sharing and nurturing a stronger sense of humanity. Practical hands-on experience and cultivation will eventually replace dependence on supermarket monopolies and their tasteless food of mysterious origins. The key lies in the students: to grow as themselves, but to also grow up and get growing. To face the realities of environmental threats and disengagement with natural processes. There is room for hope if we can change young people's attitudes towards food and each other and divert their mental energy towards other ends.

Blood orange spring salad:

This recipe is perfect for spring, the season of change and of fresh growth. Its earthy but sweet taste is down-to-earth and encouraging. Everything can be grown in the garden apart from the citrus fruits, which add an essential bit of vitality.

Ingredients:

4 blood oranges (or normal oranges
– the colour just isn't as rich!);
sliced into centimetres
4 carrots; grated
3 beetroots; left raw, sliced thinly
1 ½ courgette (optional); sliced thinly
7 large leaves of spinach;
sliced thinly
A handful of mint; roughly chopped
Juice of one lemon; pips removed
2 or 3 tbsp olive oil
1 tsp cinnamon
1 ½ tsp cumin
Salt and pepper

To make:

Mix spices and seasoning into oil and stir until blended.
Add vegetables and combine evenly.
Sprinkle with lemon juice and serve.

Sustainable society cake

I **Simon Goldsmith**

I Principled Sustainability

> Recipes are essentially a set of instructions that bring elements together to create something which is more than the sum of the individual parts. The process of making the recipe should be enjoyable and creative.

I have followed many recipes in my life, producing delicious food to share with others. The recipe I have created below is something that we should all want to share, make and enjoy the results of with as many people as possible.

I hope you find it nourishing for you, your community and the amazing planet we are fortunate to live upon.

A few years ago in Sweden I was taught the principles for this recipe and worked with people from around the world to help perfect it. It is based upon a framework that helps us understand how to live and work in a sustainable way. It helps us define what sustainability is and how to achieve it through an understanding of the elements that are essential to create a common language and set of actions. This is known as the Framework for Strategic Sustainable Development (The Natural Step) and I have made this into a recipe to illustrate how it works.

The Framework for Strategic Sustainable Development recipe for making a sustainable society (cake):

Ingredients:

- A clear applicable sustainability framework to follow
- An agreed vision of a sustainable society
- A shared language so that all 'cooks' clearly understand the key elements of the ingredients and recipe
- All the stakeholders you have in your cupboard (from a handful to billions)
- A selection of sustainability learning and collaboration techniques
- Clear scientific basis of issues (e.g. only a digestible pinch of the First Law of Thermodynamics (nothing disappears) and the Second Law of Thermodynamics (everything spreads)
- Champions from the top to the bottom
- Flexibility to adapt technologies and innovations that allow modifications to the recipe, that will make it even more successful and tasty in the future
- A healthy dollop of return on investment
- Compelling storytellers that will help the recipe spread around the world
- Inspirational leadership from a chef, restaurant team or a world full of cooks
- Optimism and motivation (this should grow organically)
- One sun.

Adjust ingredient quantities to suit an organisation/group/household/planet.

This can also be made into individual portions, please adapt the recipe as required. Where possible seek low impact ingredients, such as organic, local and fairtrade, reuse or recycle elements where possible.

To make:

First, select your framework. For this recipe I will be using the Framework for Strategic Sustainable Development (FSSD), which sets the vision and requirements of a clearly defined sustainable society. Then in a bowl appropriate to the size of cake you are making (household, community, company, country or if you have a bowl large enough, the Earth), take your stakeholders, recognising that they all have different needs but all share the same want (sustainability). Enable them to learn a shared language of what sustainability is and what all the ingredients are, to avoid confusion and align actions. Help these stakeholders understand the key requirements (including a pinch of scientific certainty) that they will need to be aware of using appropriate learning methods. This will allow your stakeholders to apply sustainability decisions to ensure the cake will be successful. It will also help them produce their own sustainability recipes.

You will add some of your champions now. These will include people from the bottom to the top of the organisation including those that make strategic decisions and can carry out actions. This will ensure that the cake will have the flavour of sustainability throughout it and that it will provide sufficient richness.

Other champions can also be added, these will include those that will head up teams that will implement sustainability through different layers of the cake and those that will rise up from the bottom of the mixture. Compelling storytellers and communicators will help share some of the ideas and create innovative new sustainable products and services that will bubble up as the cake bakes. The stakeholders will be motivated by the sustainability vision (combining the essences of pragmatism and realism) they share and create a more meaningful and fulfilling relationship with the other ingredients.

The magic of this recipe is that it does not need to be put in the oven. All the energy it needs to bake comes from the sun. It is important, however, that the temperature should not be artificially adjusted by adding carbon dioxide and please avoid adding any persistent artificial chemicals that can make the cake poisonous and ultimately lifeless.

This cake now can be left to its own devices ensuring it maintains its goal focus. It should remain wholesome, healthy and will not deteriorate if these ingredients have been used and the recipe followed. It is a cake that you can enjoy, every minute of the day and it won't put inches on your waist.

Taewa Maori

| Stephen FitzHerbert

| University of Auckland

Aotearoa[1] is the place where you can find *taewa Maori*, Maori potatoes (*Solanum tuberosum*). These arrived in Aotearoa over two hundred years ago.

Originating from Peru and Chile, they were among thousands of potato varieties found in the Andes, the outcome of generations of self-selection. There are different stories about how and what got these tubers into the soil of Aotearoa, but their entry signifies a junction where people, cultures and things came together to constitute a different relationship and dialogue between culture and nature. However they cropped up, certainly Maori – the indigenous people of Aotearoa – adopted potatoes with a zest illustrated by their vow to be *kaitiaki* or guardian of *taewa* and attributed to them the status of *taonga* or treasure[2]. Potatoes were grown almost everywhere and soon displaced other traditional root crops. *Taewa* were disease-hardy, had prolific yields, assured an abundant, nutritious food supply, and proved invaluable for trade.

The arrival, appearance and taste of the potatoes informed the names and significance Maori gave to them. *Taewa Maori* is a generic name given by some Maori *iwi* (tribes) to the many varieties of this plant and its tubers. Other names bestowed by different *iwi* and modified by dialect, include *peruperu*, *riwai* or *parareka* and there are many other names for distinct varieties that reflect their unique physical appearance and taste. A *kaumatua* (Maori elder) tells the story of one humble potato, a *karuparera* (or *kowiniwini*). This roughly translates as 'eyes of a duck'. Its skin is deep purple and marked with eye-shaped yellow patches. The *kaumatua* explain that this potato has its own *mauri* or life force and that with these eyes sees... in every direction. It is grown today, to 'keep its eyes open'. As the *kaumatua* explains, these eyes 'have seen our past, see us now and [see] what will be next... they connect us to our ancestors and if they are kept alive they will see our future generations as they too... see us'. *Karuparera* are just one of many *taewa Maori*. To their growers each demonstrates different connections and relations that constitute its own particular life force. As my Maori mentor asserts, 'we [Maori] do not own *taewa*... we are the *kaitiaki*, the guardians of *taewa*'. This is an important distinction. Maori view themselves and all other living things as born from the land, a land shared not owned.

Taewa have survived a chequered history. Over time their circulation has both flourished and retreated. Its lows can

---

[1] This is the Maori term for New Zealand.

[2] Roskruge N, Puketapu A, McFarlane T. *Nga porearea me nga matemate o nga mara taewa: pests and diseases of taewa* (Maori Potato) crops. Palmerston North: Massey University; 2010.

be mapped against periodic biophysical phenomena such as frosts, droughts and excess rain and/or related insect, and outbreaks of viruses and bacteria. Many people also claim that British colonisation, the New Zealand land wars and confiscation of Maori land and their ramifications upon Maori are at the root of its overall decline starting around 170 years ago; at the same time, the lows also express a cultural resistance and vibrancy which have ensured that *taewa* and its relationships have lived on despite adversity. Today that renaissance is evident in that *taewa* are now being grown, seed-banked, studied, storied and shared among Maori as well as *pakeha* (New Zealand Europeans). Today *taewa* are again located at a precarious junction. *Taewa* are still alive, they are still a *taonga* and Maori remain *kaitiaki*. *Taewa* contribute to keeping Aotearoa living by connecting Maori to their ancestors and helping them revive customs, stories and knowledge. Guided by these customs and accounts, *taewa* are creating new stories and knowledge.

Today, however, an insect invader again threatens their extinction, posing many difficult and contradictory questions and generating many different types of response. Potato psyllids have breached Aotearoa's bio-security borders to spread and feed on potato plants, drastically cutting yields and leaving almost nothing for seed, let alone to eat. Growers have lost one, two and even three seasons of their entire *taewa* crop and face uncertainty as to the growing of *taewa* again or to stop growing completely. As some growers concede, 'it's too heartbreaking'; 'other crops will put food on the table'; 'we have nothing to show our investors'; and 'insecticide sprays are too expensive' and/or 'insecticide sprays contravene custom'. Natural threats are rocking cultural and political-human worlds. Maori and *taewa* face significant challenges and have no attractive options for an easy way out.

This account is not a Maori recipe. The translations of Maori words are loose and do not plumb the depth of their full meaning. This account is my interpretation of *taewa Maori*, informed and inspired by conversations with Maori people and encounters with these particular potatoes. This is not a trivial point: what is in and around food is always more than just its chemicals. I hope by sharing this brief account that the reader gets an understanding of the significance of *taewa Maori* and the rich but no less contested worlds these things co-constitute at the junction between culture and nature.

Penupenu: mashed *tutaekuri* and watercress:

Ingredients:
4 or 5 *tutaekuri* (potatoes)
Milk and butter for mashing
Watercress
Sour cream
Salt and pepper

To make:
Take four or five medium sized *tutaekuri* or purple potatoes and place in a pot of boiling water. Boil till soft then drain water. Mash *tutaekuri*, adding milk and butter, mixing to desired consistency. To accompany the potatoes, boil watercress till wilted. Eat together. For *kinaki* or seasoning add sea salt and coarse pepper and add some sour cream.

Tasting wine

I **Professor Kathleen Burk**
I Department of History, UCL

There are two different ways of approaching wine: just drinking it, or tasting it.

Naturally it is possible to combine the two, but the former is the more usual approach. Yet you can vastly increase the pleasure of drinking it if you taste it first. For me 'tasting' means paying attention to what you are drinking in a structured way. This can be done reasonably unobtrusively. Here is a brief outline of how you can learn about a light – that is, unfortified – wine.

There are three actions involved in tasting wine: looking at it, smelling it, and tasting it. You can tell a lot by just looking at the wine. First of all, what is its colour? In a red wine, the more ruby-coloured it is, the younger it is; as wine gets older, it will modulate to dark cherry to garnet to amber, and, finally, to brown, by which time it will almost certainly be undrinkable. For white wine, the paler it is, the younger it is; it might also mean that it comes from a cooler climate. In any case, as it ages, it becomes darker yellow. However, just to complicate matters, a darker yellow can also indicate that it has been oaked.

Next, stick your nose deeply into the glass. First sniff it without swirling it, which allows one set of aromas to emerge; then swirl it briefly and sniff again. Does it smell of mushrooms

or other unpleasant odours (probably corked or otherwise off) or Madeira (oxidised)? If so, throw it out. Do not try to cook with corked wine – concentrated by cooking, it will make your dish taste foul. Oxidised wine, if it does not smell too bad, might be used in cooking. Is the aroma floral (possibly young Riesling, or a number of others), or nettles and perhaps gooseberries (Sauvignon Blanc), or rose petals (Gewürztraminer), or oak (white Burgundy or Chardonnay from a number of places), or petrol and honey (old Riesling)? Perhaps it smells of tar and roses, or spice (Syrah/Shiraz), or damp farmyard (old Claret), or blackcurrants (New World Cabernet Sauvignon), or lots of fruit (Merlot)? These suggestions are hardly exhaustive, or even always correct. But they are a start. A nose of lots of fruit is normally younger; with increasing age, the fruit might evolve into non-fruit aromas. If you wonder whether sniffing a wine tells you much, try drinking it whilst holding your nose, and see how little you taste.

And finally comes tasting it. Hold the wine in your mouth for a bit before swallowing it. How much prickly acid can you feel? If it is red wine, are there tannins? If you do not know what tannins are, drink some cold tea and feel what this does to your gums: that grip comes from tannin. The tannins and the acid together provide the structure of a wine: without both, a red wine feels limp, and certainly will not last. White wine will not contain tannins, but it must have acid, for the same reason. How

alcoholic is it? Is it light in your mouth, medium, or full-bodied? What are you tasting: fruit, minerals (which I occasionally refer to as stones in my own mind), or other scents and flavours? You can break the tastes down if you want, which many people love to do: cherries in Valpolicella, raspberries in red Burgundy – there are endless possibilities. Then swallow it. For how long does the flavour linger in your mouth? The single most important indicator of quality in wine is the length of the finish.

And what have you accomplished? Of course you can enjoy wine which is relatively inexpensive, and more expensive wine is not necessarily better wine – it is just that the chances are increased. But the thing about wine is that it combines intellectual challenge and alluring taste. Think about it, and then drink it.

There are no bad foods

| **Professor David A Bender**
| Emeritus Professor of Nutritional Biochemistry, UCL

Current guidelines on what constitutes a healthy diet are very clear: fat should provide only 30% of calories (and saturated fat should provide only 10%), carbohydrates 55% of calories (and sugars only 10%) and the remainder should come from protein (and perhaps 1% from alcohol).

Does this mean that so-called junk foods that are high in fat, saturated fat and sugar should be demonised and never eaten? The answer must be a resounding no! The guidelines are for your overall diet, not for individual foods. Of course, if your diet consists of burgers and chips at every meal, then it will be an unhealthy diet, but there is nothing wrong with an occasional burger. Life would be very dull if we always ate our potatoes boiled or baked, and never had them roasted or fried. Equally, life might be very short if we ate fried potatoes with every meal.

The problem is translating the nutritional guidelines into a sensible or prudent pattern of eating – making suitable choices of foods to create a balanced and healthy diet. The Food Standards Agency has designed a balanced plate

(now called the 'eatwell plates') to help people select a healthy diet – my version is shown below.

The idea of the balanced plate is that the two groups of foods that should make up the bulk of the diet are shown at the top, in the two largest segments of the plate.

On the left are fruits and vegetables. These provide vitamins, minerals and dietary fibre, as well as antioxidants and other compounds that provide protection against cancer and heart disease. Even better, fruits and vegetables provide relatively few calories, relatively little fat and most of that fat is unsaturated ("good fat" rather than "bad" saturated fat). We should aim for five servings of fruit and vegetables a day.

On the right are the starchy foods that should be providing most of our calories – bread, pasta and other cereal products and potatoes. Potatoes are not just a source of carbohydrate; they also provide dietary fibre, vitamin C and a modest amount of protein. Bread (especially wholemeal bread) is a source of dietary fibre, minerals and B vitamins – and about 14% of the calories in bread come from protein. Cakes and biscuits are included in the cereal products, but beware – they are also high in sugar and fat. Equally, some breakfast cereals might more correctly be classified as sweets because of their high sugar content.

The lower one-third of the plate contains three groups of foods that we should eat in moderation. The smallest section is in the middle – foods that are high in fat and/or sugar. This group is mainly oils and fat spreads (butter and margarine), sweetened drinks and jams. As a healthier alternative to butter and margarine a wide range of low fat spreads are available, some with as little as 20% fat (compared with 80% in butter or margarine) – and many of these are rich in ("good") polyunsaturated fats. We don't need any sugar (but it tastes good), but we do need 25 – 30% of our calories to come from fats and oils (including the hidden fat in meat and baked goods) in order to absorb the fat-soluble vitamins.

The segment on the left of the lower third of the plate is what we would regard as the traditional protein foods – meat, fish, eggs and pulses. As well as protein, meat provides iron and vita-mins, but can be high in fat. Fish, and especially oily fish such as salmon and herrings, is not only a source of protein and vitamins, but also beneficial omega-3 fats. We should aim to eat one or two fish meals a week – but remember that oily fish does not mean cod deep fried in batter. There is nothing wrong with deep fried fish occasionally, but remember that it takes up part of your "allowance" of oils and fats. Pulses (beans, peas, lentils, etc) are a good source of protein, dietary fibre and vitamins and minerals. Many people choose to eat a vegetarian diet, avoiding meat and fish, and they are perfectly healthy – equally, people who do eat meat and fish are no less healthy than vegetarians.

The final segment of the plate is milk and dairy foods – cheese and yoghurts. These are important as a source of protein, calcium and vitamins, especially vitamin B2. They can also be high in fat, so it would be sensible to choose skimmed or semi-skimmed milk, low fat cheese and yoghurt. However, there is nothing wrong with full fat cheese in moderation.

My take-away message is that if you have a good mixed diet, eating the various groups of foods from the balanced plate in appropriate amounts, then there are no individual bad foods.

This is a performance after all

| **Vipul Sangoi and Anusha Subramanyam**
| Beeja Co.

Beeja means 'seed' in Hindi. Seeing a tiny seedling emerge from a dry and wrinkled seed and watching its growth and transformation, is to observe the mystery of life unfold.

We are fascinated by nature, biology, and the particular internal architecture of a seed. It is a matter of changes of scale. A seed allows us to move further inside, to examine its structure, to go up and down, both vertically and horizontally; once you see beyond a seed, you can see a leaf, a tree, a forest and the whole ecology.

In keeping with its name, Beeja aims to generate new ideas, new understanding and fresh creative forms, particularly through the way that it allows us to be alert to, and take tremendous pleasure in living organisms and biological webs of relatedness. Like a seed underneath the soil collecting all sorts of nutrients, Beeja works as a collective and draws on the skills of its members to develop a distinctive way of working that offers an all-round experience. It is about life's choreography.

In the case of *Bharatanatyam* dance, it is a composite art form drawing on rich traditions of Indian poetry, devotion, drama, philosophy, myth and visual

Chana palak dal:

Ingredients:

200g *Chana dal* (use yellow spilt *dal* if unavailable)
400g fresh spinach - thoroughly washed and finely chopped
2 medium sized tomatoes - blanched - roughly chopped
4 garlic cloves - finely chopped
small piece of ginger - skinned and finely sliced or chopped
2-3 green chillies sliced down the middle
2 tbsp vegetable or sunflower oil
1/2 tsp mustard seeds
1 tsp cumin (*jeera*) seeds
1/2 tsp turmeric powder
2 tsp coriander cumin (*dhaanajeera*) powder
1-1.5 tsp salt (to taste)

1 pressure cooker - highly recommended (for all types of Indian cooking)

To make:

Soak the *dal* in warm water for 1 hour. Add the *dal* with spinach and place in pressure cooker with 750ml of water. Cook until tender. In a separate pan heat the oil. Add the mustard seed and wait for them to start popping. Add cumin seeds. After 30 seconds add ginger and garlic. After 1 minute add tomatoes and chillies. After another minute of stirring add the turmeric and coriander cumin powder. Add this mixture to the *dal* and spinach. Give it a good stir. Add salt to taste.

Add boiling water to the *dal* if the mix is very thick. Cook a few more minutes to blend the flavours. This dish can be had as a soup or made slightly thicker and eaten together with chapatis, naan, pita bread or bread.

art. The dancer uses eyes and hand gestures to sculpt the physical space around her and lead the audience into an imaginative realm of story and emotion. As with any collaborative effort, we endeavour to explore a unified and coherent performance form to integrate languages, music and body movements. What binds them is the rhythm and beats which create a structure that every single aspect can follow. *Bharatanatyam* performance is a dialogue between the dancer, musicians and the audience, creating a dynamic of presence and immediacy. We constantly work around it; we are dancing through moments of life to embrace something with all its messiness and imperfection, to be responsive to all the complexities with love and passion. This leads to our shared interest in cooking.

We are both vegetarians but for different reasons: one is deeply influenced by spirituality; the other is for environmental reasons. Nevertheless, we both believe in non-violence and the ethics of care. We both take cooking as another kind of performing art to express and share our values, identity and feelings. We enjoy dancing, food and life: all three are connected. That is, the liminal, contingent, and ephemeral investigations that we undertake as performance and visual artists provides the impetus for similar production in our cooking.

We are happily creating our kitchen choreography. Since we come from different parts of India, we have inherited quite different traditions of cuisine. While Southern cuisine emphasizes the bounty of the tropics, like using many varieties of rice and protein-rich pulses, Western cuisine does the same but in a very different way. Both of us also share a common ground in the food of the North which centres on a variety of breads. We try to develop the complexity of our recipes by adding such classic spices as mustard seeds, cloves, cumin, ginger, cardamom as well as experimenting with new ingredients. Ingredients are only one part of the story of course. Ideas for preparation naturally accompanied the constituents themselves. Again, we constantly work with what is available, which, in a city like London, is expanding all the time. It literally took us five years to get a recipe right, to work out a system and a balance. It is this rich mosaic – each piece related but distinct – that we both desire to perform well. To give an example, in an Indian household, not only can you

smell the food in the kitchen but you can hear sounds too. We can know roughly what someone is cooking by listening to the sounds in the kitchen.

Both dancing and cooking are performance arts, uplifted by an appreciative audience. We have always been interested in the seeds from which whole organisms can be regenerated. Seeds inspire us by their scale of change and transformation, their continual change of form towards a more desirable present and future.

Towards a co-operative society

I Dr. Mary Hilson

I Department of Scandinavian Studies, UCL

Co-operative societies may be formed for many different reasons but they seem to be particularly well-suited to the production and distribution of basic foodstuffs.

Whether it was the Danish farmer delivering milk to the local *andelsmejeri* (co-operative dairy), or the British housewife buying her groceries and collecting her 'divi' from the 'Co-op', co-operatives seem to have flourished best of all as a way to help ordinary people of limited

means to secure their basic needs. Some of the large urban co-operatives that came to dominate the cities of Europe in the twentieth century, like the Helsinki co-operative Elanto, started out as bakeries, for what could be more fundamental than the supply of bread?

The International Co-operative Alliance estimates that over 1 billion people are currently members of co-operative societies around the world. Given the inevitable diversity of co-operatives in different times and places, it is perhaps difficult to find a common recipe for a successful co-operative society. At its most basic level 'co-operation' simply means 'working together'. Although there are many different ways of co-operating, many co-operative societies define themselves with reference to one particular model: that of the Rochdale Equitable Society of Pioneers, founded in 1844 and widely copied throughout northern Europe and beyond. In the 1930s, Rochdale was the starting point for the International Co-operative Alliance as it attempted to establish a common set of principles for the movement[1]. In a statement agreed upon at the 1937 International Co-operative Congress in London, the four essential ingredients of a co-operative society were listed as follows:

- Open membership: co-operatives were to be open to all, regardless of class, race, sex, religion, etc.
- Democratic control: co-operatives were managed by a board elected on

the basis of one member one vote.

- Distribution of the surplus to the members in proportion to their transactions (often known, at least in the UK, as the 'divi' or dividend).
- Limited interest on capital: in this respect co-operatives were considered to be fundamentally different to conventional businesses, because they had no obligation to return a profit to their shareholders.

In addition, the conference noted three extra principles which were not considered essential for membership of the ICA but which were nonetheless important:

- Political and religious neutrality
- Cash trading
- Promotion of education, usually by setting aside a proportion of the trading surplus for this end.

The principles have been revised twice since, but remain in essence the same[2].

In some ways the co-operative movement is unusual in having such a clear statement of its guiding principles. It is hard to think of a similar defining statement for the socialist labour movement, for example, even though it had no shortage of founding texts.

Nonetheless, this is only the basic recipe, and there are many different variations on it throughout the world. Above all, what seems to have divided co-operators is the desired balance between pragmatism and idealism. Was co-operation simply a successful business model – albeit one that was radically different from the capitalist model – or was it a social movement founded on the aspiration to change the world, and replace the current competitive society with a 'Co-operative Commonwealth'? Should co-operation be regarded as the 'third pillar' of the labour movement, like the famous socialist co-operative society Vooruit of Gent, in Belgium, or was it strictly politically neutral, as the powerful consumer co-operatives of Scandinavia insisted? For many people, co-operation was always literally about bread and butter (and also of course coffee, tea, raisins, macaroni, sugar, oatmeal, flour, etc.). But precisely because these goods are so important, there were also those who insisted – and still do – that the salvation of society lay in the co-operative organisation of their production and supply.

[1] Mary Hilson, "A Consumers' International? The International Cooperative Alliance and Cooperative Internationalism 1918-1939: A Nordic Perspective," *International Review of Social History*, 56 (2011), 203-233.

[2] Statement on the Co-operative identity. (http://www.ica. coop/coop/principles.html). Accessed 5/7/2011.

Urban food and sustainable cities

I **Dr. Ian Scott**
I UCL Grand Challenges

Most city-dwellers, especially in wealthy industrialised countries, have little or no connection to the countryside and farming. How food crops are grown, or animals raised for meat, are subjects remote from the daily life and preoccupations of people in big towns and cities.

In the UK now, most food shopping is done in supermarkets, much of it on the basis of a weekly or fortnightly visit by car and a quick whizz around the aisles with a large trolley. People, as ever, enjoy their food, but busy lives mean that its acquisition has to be rapid and efficient. At home, time constraints and modern life-styles have conspired to increase the demand for 'convenience foods' and ready meals – factors that further isolate the consumer from food in its natural, unprocessed, state.

Labels indicating 'farm fresh' have a certain validity – supply chains have become incredibly efficient over the years – but don't do anything to enhance consumer interest in and engagement with the origins of food. We complacently get what we want, whenever we want it, but – in my view – the *Food Junctions*

initiative has stimulated and marshalled a strong sense that food can be a whole lot more interesting and central to our health and wellbeing.

Jamie Oliver, a great champion of healthy eating, has made a hugely important contribution to the national debate on food. As he says in his 2005 manifesto, more should be done to spread the message that eating a healthy school meal is a great foundation for a kid's education and future health. For my money, it's the mindset and interests of children that should be the greatest priority. Raised on a farm in Somerset in the 1950s and 60s, I took no conscious interest in vegetable gardening – my father was too busy milking cows, raising chickens and growing grass and cereal crops, and I had to help him after school. But years working in cities have given me a strong drive to grow my own food, and so I have tried, wherever I've lived, to cultivate my own fruit and vegetables, whether on a windowsill in a block of flats in Finland or in my current back garden in an English country town. I like to produce my own food not only because it tastes great and reduces the size of the family's weekly bill for food, but also because growing it gives me great personal contentment. In modern terms, it enhances my wellbeing. For a few hours every weekend I'm at one with nature in my suburban vegetable plot.

Farmers and horticulturalists apart, people in the UK who grow their own

food are mostly engaged in it as a lifestyle choice. But for the vast majority of the planet's population, whether in rural areas, small towns or the huge mega-cities of the Global South, the capacity to grow a few vegetables can make a huge difference to their quality of life, and indeed their very survival. Oxfam's Grow campaign, announced on 31 May 2011, highlights the vital importance of movements, whether global, or local, like *Food Junctions*, that are in the vanguard of showing us, of all generations, better ways to live our lives and care for the Earth.

Urban rural linkage

I Ailbhe Gerrard
I Social Farm

This adventure started, as many do, with a vision.

I was researching urban agriculture's potential to feed people in one of Europe's largest cities – London. It was fascinating investigating international cities' experiences in growing food on periurban and urban land from Cuba to Saint Petersburg. My urban agriculture research included a critical analysis of conventional agriculture, and led to an urge to engage in a practical experiment: linking the urban and the rural through low carbon food growing using perennial crops. So last year, back I went to my roots in rural Ireland and found and bought a little farm of 65 acres.

The farm is almost perfectly situated, a lovely piece of landscape on Lough Derg which is a fresh water lake of 118 square kilometres, dotted with islands and surrounded by hills. The land I have flows down from a little hill (80 metres above sea level) covered with 15 year old oak, ash, and beech plantation, through gently sloping west-facing fields to the lake shore (40 metres above sea level). The farm is bordered by two streams at either boundary and has two mysterious and fabulous large circles of ancient beech trees.

So what am I doing now? I am sharefarming with an experienced tillage farmer for most of the farm (45 acres) to gain farming experience. We have sown 45 acres with spring barley, and over time I plan to swap some of this tillage land over to pasture. Despite my concerns about conventional arable farming, it is an amazing sight to watch the tillage fields turning from brown soil to a green germinating mist to a deep luxuriant green.

Right now I am busy thinning and pruning the 15 acres of forest plantation (using vegetable oil in the chainsaws and horse logging) which will make the forest much more lovely to walk in, and will produce a lot of wood for fuel. I have also started planting a vegetable garden, and have reseeded and fenced paddocks so two horses (cattle, sheep and maybe pigs to come) can graze down the pastures (about 6 acres). I am making links with local farmers, inhabitants and food growers to see what potential we have to collaborate and am learning a lot about organic horticulture, agroforestry, perennial plants for food and local food networks. I am observing the land over a one year cycle before designing and planting permanent tree crops or putting in infrastructure, apart from an obligatory cattle crush.

The next step is to link back to the urban. I am an urban/rural hybrid myself, like many Irish people. There is a group of urban artists and researchers interested in coming to visit the farm and a lot of interest generally in sustainable food production. As the farm is only two

hours' drive from Dublin, and one hour from Limerick and Galway, I am planning to share my farming experience and farm produce with urban friends and interested people. Through this linkage we may be in a better position to re-imagine the urban and the rural. Eventually the lake and river system might become the main route to the farm, as in pre-oil times when farm produce was loaded onto boats at dozens of little stone harbours around the lake to be shipped to towns and cities.

As I was arranging to buy the farm last autumn, I noticed the forest had dozens of wild cherry trees planted on the southern fringe. I picked handfuls of small, sweet, juicy, finger-staining dark cherries and planned a delicious cherry crumble when I finally owned the farm. Here is a recipe for this celebratory cherry crumble dessert, which I am looking forward to making this autumn when the cherries are ripe again. Come and join me!

Ailbhe's wild cherry crumble recipe:

Ingredients:

1 kg wild cherries
50-70g local honey
150g plain organic flour
100g Irish summer butter
Handful of organic oat flakes
75g light brown organic sugar
A few tablespoons linseed/flax seed/muesli for top scattering if you wish.

To make:

Gather some friends and stone the cherries (You can also choose to leave the stones in and ask people to spit the stones out as they eat and collect them). Put the cherries in a large shallow baking dish and pour the honey on top. Rub the butter and flour together with your finger tips until it reaches breadcrumb texture, then add the sugar and toss in the oak flakes. Scatter the crumble lightly over the fruit and add linseed/ flax seed or muesli on top if desired.

Bake in a preheated oven at 200C / 400F or Gas 6 for thirty five minutes, or until the top is crisp and golden and some purple juices may have bubbled up through the crumble. Serve with thick pouring cream or yoghurt.

Woolton Pie

| Dr. Richard Farmer

| Film Studies, UCL Centre for Intercultural Studies

During the Second World War, the problems associated with international shipping – not least the constant danger of U-boat attack – meant that the amount of food imported into Britain fell dramatically. Given that before the war British larders had often been filled with foreign-produced food, this brought about rapid and far-reaching changes to the national diet.

The Ministry of Food (MoF) was placed in charge of an extensive rationing scheme which controlled how much meat, cheese, butter, tea and sugar, to give but a few examples, each person could purchase.

The MoF's work was not limited to simply restricting consumption. It was also engaged in a battle to keep Britons fighting fit, and there seems to be some truth in the belief that Britain was healthier – if sometimes hungrier – during the war than it was before or has been since. Vegetables were crucial to this project because of their nutri-

tional value. Cabbage and carrots were tirelessly boosted for their health-giving properties, with the latter being said to help people see better in the Blackout.

What's more, because British-grown vegetables contributed to the war effort by leaving more shipping space for guns and tanks, Britons were encouraged to grow their own food by the justly famous 'Dig for Victory' campaign. Food became, in the words of a Ministry slogan, a vital 'munition of war.' Potatoes were perhaps the most widely promoted vegetable, not least because they provided a filling and patriotic alternative to bread, much of which was baked with imported wheat. The lengths to which the MoF went in order to boost the humble spud is perhaps best demonstrated by a festival held on Oxford Street in December 1942, where Father Christmas handed out baked potatoes to visitors instead of presents.

Vast sums of money were spent on providing British cooks with new vegetable recipes – anyone for devilled potatoes or farmhouse scramble? As well as telling the British people what to eat, MoF propaganda also tried to teach them how to cook it. Newspaper advertisements, radio shows and short films all insisted that if vitamins were to be preserved, cabbage should be cooked for no more than 15 minutes, which begs the question of how long it was being boiled for before. Similar instructions were issued for other vegetables. It became as difficult to avoid the Ministry's propaganda as it was to avoid the food controls it administered, meaning that the MoF became as important to the culture of wartime Britain as it was to its dining tables. Food was central to the national experience of the war, and helped shape British national identity in this period.

Overseeing the whole operation was Lord Woolton, an avuncular figure who served to humanise what might otherwise have been an arithmetical and impersonal system. Woolton remained a hugely popular figure throughout his time as Minister of Food and lent his name to a number of ersatz dishes in which British-grown vegetables were substituted for more hard-to-come-by imported foodstuffs. The most famous of these dishes was Woolton Pie, a dish described by one wag as being just like a steak and kidney pie – but without the steak and kidney.

Although Woolton Pie never achieved the same level of popularity with the British public as the man for which it was named, it is an intriguing recipe nonetheless, demonstrating as it does some of the ways in which the war affected Britain's food and also the eagerness with which the Ministry of Food attempted to keep the British people healthy, well-fed and well-informed. It is interesting to speculate about whether a government's attempts to control diet would be as well received today as they were between 1939 and 1945.

Woolton Pie:

Recipe as given in the House of Commons, 29 April 1941

To make:

Take one pound (450g) each diced of potatoes, cauliflower, swedes, and carrots, three or four spring onions, if possible, one tea-spoonful of vegetable extract and one tablespoonful of oatmeal. Cook all together for 10 minutes with just enough water to cover. Stir occasionally to prevent the mixture from sticking. Allow to cool, put into a pie dish, sprinkle with chopped parsley and cover with a crust of potato or wheatmeal pastry. Bake in a moderate oven until the pastry is nicely browned and serve hot with a brown gravy.

[NB – ingredients can be varied according to the vegetables in season.]

Word of mouth

| Professor Ian Needleman
| UCL Eastman Dental Institute

I would like to explore the relationships between food and the mouth, and offer you a practical 'experiment' to do at home to emphasise these.

What closer connection can there be than between food and the mouth? Food has a big impact on maintaining good oral health and good oral health clearly affects what and how well we eat. But of course there is much more than this. Both the mouth and food have very strong emotional and cultural links and these are often inseparable from the more scientific or clinical aspects.

In terms of food for good oral health there are a few simple guides to consider:

Sugar and tooth decay

- Sugar fuels the bacteria in your mouth to produce acid which can eventually cause decay.
- Sugar is sugar. The bacteria in your mouth are not sophisticated and can't tell the difference between refined and natural sugar.
- Lots of sugar vs. little sugar. Even a small amount of sugar provides fuel for the bacteria to produce acid.
- How to be clever. The number of times a day that you take sugar is the most important element (no matter how little each time). Cheat the bacteria and enjoy sugar at meal times (within a few minutes) and you are unlikely to have a problem.
- Artificial sweeteners cannot cause decay

Acids and tooth erosion

- Similar to tooth decay, frequent acidic food and drink during the day will eventually leave their toll on the teeth. Erosion is the latest so-called 'dental epidemic', particularly in younger people. The acids slowly take away the outer layer of the tooth, and the results can be unsightly, leave the teeth very sensitive and uncomfortable and weaken them.

- Acidic food and drink include citrus fruit and juices, colas and white wine. However, any carbonated drink will be acidic due to the dissolved gas turning to acid within the drink.
- The key is not really abstention, but limiting the number of times during the day and how long the teeth are bathed in the acid each time. In other words, a single acidic drink sipped slowly over an hour is likely to be more damaging than the same drunk over a few minutes.
- A further tip is not to brush within one hour of taking the acid to give time for the tooth to harden up again.

Food and gum health

There are many claims for detergent foods that naturally cleanse teeth. Unfortunately, they are not really effective and no substitute for great oral hygiene. In terms of maintaining gum health, a good balanced diet is all that is needed in relation to food considerations.

Food, oral health and wellbeing: A practical experiment with chocolate truffles

If you need any convincing about the importance of good food to oral health and wellbeing, just try this very easy and quick recipe. The pleasure in making them, especially as a team effort, is only exceeded by the sensation of the chocolate melting in your mouth.

Chocolate truffles:

Ingredients:
250g 70% cocoa chocolate. Grate by hand or in a food processor
200ml double cream
150g caster sugar
Cocoa powder

To make:
Mix cream and caster sugar in a glass bowl and heat in stages in a microwave until hot. I suggest giving one-minute bursts, carefully mixing and then checking if hot. Once hot, add the chocolate and mix thoroughly.
Leave to cool, cover and refrigerate overnight.
Use a teaspoon to scoop the mixture and roll into a ball.
Roll in cocoa powder.
Share and eat.

Epilogue

| Lukas Meusburger

| Department of Economics, UCL

This *Cookbook* has been with me for almost two years now. I did not know at the time that there would be a *Cookbook*, but it is clear now that there was always going to be one – as the logical outcome of a communal journey. We spent a lot of time preparing and organising *Food Junctions* throughout the whole academic year 2009/2010. Often enough it was the library instead of the pub on a Friday night. I did sometimes ask myself why I was doing all this. The relatively inflexible curriculum of the undergraduate course I was studying at that time did not make the matter easier either. I would not say that we were ever close to giving up, but there were, of course, times when we could not see the end of this huge undertaking.

In these situations it was often in team meetings where we managed to get our motivation back – more than once by developing even more ambitious plans. In the end, *Food Junctions* was a huge success. Many people from UCL and local community groups made the two weekends into an unforgettable event.

I did not sleep a lot on the last weekend of events which happened to be in the middle of my exam period. I was too excited, with parents and friends from Austria over in London and all of us obviously having something to celebrate. When it was finally over on Sunday night, I just fell into my bed. Probably the strangest night of my life followed. Quite literally, the whole year passed in

front of my closed eyes - from developing the first ideas around a table, to having breakdowns and breakthroughs, to finally seeing it all happen. I was not very well rested in the morning, but I was really happy. This night alone was an incredible experience!

Many things were talked about at *Food Junctions* and important topics were touched upon. But just like the events themselves, my dream passed. The impressions and memories stay of course but as time goes by, new things come to one's mind and the previous memories fade away a bit.

I quite like to write things down. It helps to focus on what is left to do and is a reminder of the decisions that have been made which, especially when working in a team, can save many hours of discussion. But more importantly, having something written down provides a foundation made up of previous thoughts and energy, on which to build in future, either along the previous lines or in new directions.

I think this is one thing this book can do. It is not our or my opinion on a number of topics, but many people's stories about food and what comes along with it. I hope – and indeed believe – that this will not only help us all to remember, but will also give useful guidance for future thoughts, projects and events on the topics covered.

Our approach has always been not to comment on the contributions that we heard at *Food Junctions*, or on the ones we received for the book. We regard the audience and the readers as mature enough to think his or her own thoughts. At *Food Junctions* it was the audience who helped digest (and spice up) what was said through discussions, and I really hope that a good talk about the articles and topics with friends or colleagues will do the same in the case of the book. Writing an epilogue for this book, however, naturally gives me the privilege of having the last word and I will use the opportunity to add two things to all that has been said already.

The first has to do with change. The current economic system produces more goods than ever before, but too many people still have almost nothing. Aside from these unjust inequalities, this abundance often comes at the expense of the natural environment. A lot of the people and organisations that have been among our contributors do a lot to change things for the better, be it through their communities or by producing academic knowledge. While I think that individual or community action is good and necessary, I believe that they will not be enough. It is institutions that set the rules of the game and in many cases determine our actions. Take the case of genetically modified food. Of course you can decide not to consume these products as an individual, but as soon as you enter a restaurant or want a snack on the go, the issue becomes much harder. When these products are strictly not allowed to be sold in a country, the problem for you as an individual is resolved. I do not want to remove our responsibility for what we do and its implications but what could change a game more than changing the rules by which it is being played?

The second thing I would like to add brings us back to you and me - the individual. Many of the important topics that demand our attention like environmental degradation or poverty are complex and just cannot be tackled with easy and quick solutions. If you try to save the environment by producing all plane fuel from apparently CO_2 neutral plants, you will soon run into the problem of having less space to grow food, which will lead to rising food prices and more hunger. What I want to say is that only seeing and taking into account the whole picture can help us find solutions when we talk about topics as complex as the above.

The current industrial food system makes it possible to eat without thinking about the produce. Food being funda-

These three pictures were taken in Nicaragua. The first (p.196) shows two men searching an already harvested field in hopes of finding something edible. The second two show children receiving a free school breakfast. School breakfast projects are a common way of increasing school attendance in poor countries as they provide an incentive to send children to school. They also improve school performance because students can concentrate better with proper nourishment.

These breakfasts were initially provided in various schools in Nicaragua, financed mainly by international development projects. Due to their great success the government of Nicaragua itself started to provide such breakfasts in schools throughout the whole country, which meant that the individually financed projects could be concluded. Today about 95% of the country's schools are covered by the programme.

mental for both our wellbeing and the wellbeing of the earth should be the thing one thinks about a bit more than absolutely necessary. If one manages to identify with the food one eats on a personal level, it becomes easier to see this big picture - when you also know where it grew, how it was processed and what that means, not just how it looks in the supermarket. Furthermore, knowing something about the food you cook, makes it more fun to actually use. Think of cooking with ingredients you don't know anything about, as opposed to talking to a friend about how you grew these herbs that you are just using for a salad and how they will change the taste – which would you prefer?

Hence, to achieve the former - institutional change - we need the latter, individual change. Everyone should try to identify with the food she or he eats and think about the effect that personal choice has on the whole planet. Doing this will make a difference and also show you, as an individual, what institutional changes you want to see in order to support the ideas you stand for. We do live in a democracy where the people have some power. Who else can and should demand that institutional change if not us?

In *Food Junctions*, *Foodpaths* and this *Cookbook*, we aimed to facilitate future engagement simply by showing how much we take for granted when we eat lunch, and by revealing the immense variety of food-related topics one can engage with. We certainly all learned a lot about food culture, food politics and certainly also about ourselves but more importantly we were able to facilitate new connections between different people and groups that work on similar topics but on different fronts. Be it researchers from different disciplines who met at *Food Junctions* for the first time or a poetry group that discovered the beauty of performing in an unusual natural environment in the middle of London.

Having been through all this, it would be nice to close this *Cookbook* with the recipe to achieve these individual and institutional changes. As I see it, however, there is no simple recipe that could tell us how to do this and therefore I cannot provide it. I do know, however, that what has made this *Cookbook* into what it is, just as has been the case with the previous projects, is people's ideas and sharing them with others. This brings me back to what I said before about writing things down. Just as writing the last word does not mean that everything has been said, this *Cookbook* does not mark the end of our journey. I hereby encourage you to use this book as a collection of thoughts to build upon, to think about, to cook with and to share around a kitchen table while eating a nice self-cooked meal.

Enjoy and continue the journey!